EVOLUTIONARY ESSAYS 02

Kyle Lance Proudfoot

authorHOUSE®

AuthorHouse™ UK
1663 Liberty Drive
Bloomington, IN 47403 USA
www.authorhouse.co.uk
Phone: 0800.197.4150

Published by AuthorHouse 04/30/2015

ISBN: 978-1-5049-4186-0 (sc)
ISBN: 978-1-5049-4187-7 (e)

The Unending Finite and Infinite Complex

Though it may seem self-contradictory, now and then, both the Finite and Infinite Form's and Object's are unending, except with absolute annihilation of Existence, for Matter and Energy being convertible are both Infinite, the difference between Plato and Aristotle Form's and Object's in transition.

Energy and Matter are transmutable as Law Of Conservation Of Energy dictates.

Infinity and Near-Infinity are indeed confusing, however without an existing Infinity you can also not have GOD who is Omniscient and Omnipresent. You can also not have a perpetually expanding spherical Universe, for such would only collapse again. The ensuing destruction of all Form's, Object's and Being's in such is absurd. Does everyone and/or everybody then go to Plane of Spirit's and Soul's only? See my Evolutionary Essays – Part 01 – Published by AuthorHouse UK.

Is Plane of Spirit's and/or Soul's even spherical?

Are Body, Matter, Mind, Energy, Information, Spirit and/or Soul not actually all intertwined? From Point, Line, Spiral, Circle, Ellipse to Sphere throughout each other?

Do we not actually have an ad infinitum of multiple Planes also in the the Microcosm which are equivalent to Multi-Universes?

To state that such Planes, in Microcosm and Macrocosm, are ad infinitum and all layered on top of and through one another is *not* impossible. There is practically no other way through varying degrees of osmosis through all things, all things are interconnected though there is still distance and density. See ditto.

The Plane Theory that there are only 999 Planes Of Heaven and 666 Planes Of Hell is and how many Middle Planes is also indeterminable. It's more like that is a reduction for sake of simplicity and symbolism cause it's more like the problem in Mathematic's of also .33333333333 33333333333333333333333333333333333333333333…

What is also really 'iffy' is whether or not Existence can be destroyed, thus technically such must include the Being's, Object's and Form's which reside in such, we do not know what is outside of the Universe, thus returning again to the impossible Theory Of Absolute Nothingness which is just as loopy as Theory Of Creation. It just is and evolves continuously and perpetually, technically a duck becoming a seagull…

What we, Humanity, have here is a serious Paradox, and not just a Pandora's Box, but the worst Black Schrödinger's Cat in a Black Box Effect, between Finite and Infinite.

And the Finite, if you allow for Karma and Reincarnation, is losing badly. See next essay in 3 parts here…

You cannot deny the persistence of Cause And Effect through centuries and millennia, through nanoseconds to decades, throughout 3D Energy Matrix, or 4D Energy Matrix though I prefer to place, Nicht Ontheil Chronos, in 12th Dimension, and Zero Point Field Theory which also does not know what is *outside* of the Universe. This is P.S. nothing new under the Sun's, Moon's, Star's and Black Holes…

Is there, in fact, anything, or even anyone, original in Infinity? Yes, it's about a strongly associated with IT concept called Unique Combination; I could be the only one with 12 stripes in my hair style on Planet Earth just like I'm still the only one with my full name Kyle Lance Proudfoot though I have seen now one other Kyle Proudfoot but does this count for all of Infinity: 'There can be only one.' Quantum Science also states that each Object, Form and Being in same Space Time, or Timeline, has to be Unique.

Is there any difference between spiritual Form's and physical Form's? This cannot be by definition or it causes a major Object Violation, they simply bind with each other all the time, continuously evolving to a better and/or worse existence i.e. through Free Will I could go and crash my car on purpose and still have to pay since No Mo Insurance due to My Fault In Claim and live on peanut butter and crackers only… As I stated in Part 01 of Evolutionary Essays pls don't mind my Black Sense Of Humor which takes away from long over-complicated dryness of content.

Yet I learn and 3 years later I choose to ride a bike: 'Do Not Drink And Bike!'

No one these days, especially with IT, Sex, Drug's and Rock and Roll, can tell the difference between Reality and Unreality anymore, maybe quite literally the difference between Life and Death, we know they go somewhere but no one has evidence or proof; we are also only starting on Genetic's but such will never explain Soul and Spirit.

Theory's of black or white scenarios are retrograded and invalidated by all the degrees of different shades of gray…

Each Light casts a Shadow and all of the Light's and all of the Shadow's are woven and blended together throughout all of Space And Time, allowing for distance and density. Only pure Planes of GOD, Soul, Spirit, Light, Shadow, Nothingness and Nothing could theoretically not suffer transition and transmutation. See Buddhism.

Both Light and Shadow Energy self-propagate with only the Infinite Null Potential to stimulate Infinity. See Kinetic Energy.

What would the purpose be of GOD, God's and Goddesses, also so easily discarded by many, especially Scientist's, Religisist's, Atheist's and Anarchist's, if in the end it all just went away, at a snap of a finger, blink of an eye… Such sounds more like a stupendous Tabla Rasa scenario out of control.

In fact, would not HUMANITY not just all start committing hari-kari en masse cause it's all the worst Nietschian Annihilism, it's all futile without resistance, hopeless and nihilistic, without any purpose, as everything descends into spiracle Chaos everywhere… Are we not instead seeing these repetitious Quantum Phenomena, and not just only one time at Revelation's, but at all levels throughout millennia… For example, I liquidate a whole Ant Nest with beer in the park, is that not their Armageddon? Yet, eventually, a hell of a lot more come back to get the free sugar and multiply… We also see this with people, despite conditions in Africa their population keeps growing.

Is there no Order in Chaos and Cosmos? Would it not all fall of fly apart?

Just because something is unpredictable to the Nth Degree does not mean that there is no underlying Mathematic's governing it. You just have to figure it out, like stop smoking at 50 years old since 18 years old. It's just Stupid Human, from Ultra-Stupid Ape despite weak links in the chains, who is misinterpreting all the time, and repeatedly.

What is really a necessary Good, Neutral and/or Evil?

If one cannot climb or descend throughout the hierarchies of Known and Unknown Existence through Evolution then nothing makes sense anymore…

Saying there is no such thing as empty Space, Ether being between the Galaxy's, in the Universe is not per se incorrect, but it does not say what is *outside* of the Universe, or who… Technically speaking, once again as I have stated in my other works, if the Universe is expanding would the friction into *something* not burn it up completely causing another god awful Coffee Cup Effect.

You cannot deny the existence of Soul and Spirit anymore then you can deny the persistence of Matter, when the Body and Mind dies it's no longer animate and it does not even weigh as much! This is Science and Philosophy 101 yet is easily forgotten.

Simply or in complexity taking on a new and/or old Object, Form and Variables does not make the underlying Ideas, Causes and Effect's only Finite.

Everything changes in evolutions in existences yet there also has to be One Timeline and One Existence, otherwise there is only Nothing, however such does not take away from the infinitesimal multiplying manifold of many small matrixes of forms, expressions, ideas and information.

For example, you can implode or explode, but not the two at the same time, there is a nanosecond delay; you also have Love or Hate, though relative, does not change this Universal Principle that all things take Time. Despite being Virtual there is also a small delay for Soul and Spirit to travel dependent on density and distance as according to Einstein's Relativity Theory. Theoretically, only GOD has no delays, the Throne Of God now having to be Absolute Null Point which is either zenith or center of Universe. SATAN can, therefore, only be the Big Black Hole which the whole Universe is spiraling into and being devoured, '…devourer of souls…'

For GOD to exist must He not have Mass? Light Energy still has a small amount of Mass, it being a medium of waves and particles. Still though, if it takes only a zillionth a second to get there and build a Colony then it's a Mut Point.

Thus, once again, Nothing cannot exist, which is not a problem.

However, to add to the conundrum, all Object's, Form's and Being's which exist in Time And Space have to be Finite or Near-Infinite, therefore wrecking Immortality. One cannot exist without Mass, and that is a problem.

Therefore, there must be a Timeless Plane or there is no Infinity.

It's more like we're on a Test Field and it's buggy. Well, also a good inspiration, since when is Humanity not buggy?

To not absolutely conclude this Debate we have to submit that Only Finite with no Immortality, especially of Soul and Spirit which could theoretically be Massless or hardly any Mass at all, is falling so short of the mark, and '…no, I won't come back to this Backwater Colony Planet…', that no one can believe anymore in the temporary Nature of Existence through Evolution…

Karma And Reincarnation Is At Near-Infinite Variables

Part 1 of 3

Let's first put several points about Karma and Reincarnation in a list:

The primary quality of Karma and Reincarnation is Cause and Effect.

Karma is not dependent on Reincarnation, though Reincarnation is dependant on Karma.

Karma is a virtual quality on Object's and Being's. Being's and Object's are in certain and uncertain quantities, though each Object and Being is Unique.

Reincarnation is an event which happens sometime after the death of the Being and Object, it requires Karma to function.

The Law Of Conservation Of Energy, whether this be spiritual Energy and/or physical Energy, allows for the possibility of Karma and Reincarnation.

The actual Unique Combination of the quality and quantity of Karmas and Reincarnation's results in Near-Infinite Variables.

Karma is not per se literal, absolute or equivalent i.e. if I kick a garbage can it does not mean a garbage can will kick me; one is animate, the other is inanimate.

The reduction of the Classes of Karma into Positive Karma, Neutral Karma and Negative Karma is recommended. See Buddhism and other Philosophy's and Religion's.

The Topic of Moral's and Ethic's cannot be avoided when discussing Karma and Reincarnation, '…a stone cast into the water sends ripples and waves…'

Some foolish Mortal Human taking Karma into his or her hands is now what retribution of Karma is, such is simply revenge and only causes another vicious circle, though according to Hinduism some individuals and groups are the vessels of Karma, like a Hero or United Nation's.

Karma and Reincarnation is a Universal Principle or Universal Truth which no one and nobody is exempt from in any Plane Of Existence; the only ones who are not, do not exist, however only Nothing does not exist.

Time is bound closely with Karma and Reincarnation, '…you have to ask yourself why some Karmas take so long to manifest while they get away with bloody murder…' Well, this could happen in the Afterlife.

Karma has Memory.

Karma and Reincarnation is a natural mechanism which obeys a program. Let's call it Karma and Reincarnation Program of Universal Matrix.

1. Cause And Effect

So very many articles on Karma and Reincarnation discuss only or primarily in length Cause and Effect. I'll try to keep it short…

Particles and waves, chemicals and neuro-transmitters, fields, spirits, ideas, thoughts, words and actions all interact with each other on a continual basis getting split and bonded countless times, '…now I'm your Friend, now I'm not…' This causes new Timelines at all levels.

Each carries a certain 'weight' of positivity, neutrality and/or negativity i.e. if I yell you are a low-life Stupid Human then it depends on who, where, when, how and why it is said, such also allows for random Act's Of Anarchy which still cause new Timelines.

Newton's Law states and equal and opposite reaction, however Einstein states a 10x or greater force in return, '…why do when I kick a dog a horse shows up and kicks me in the head…'

The recipient often reacts in like fashion, though some practicing Buddhism or Christianity, depending on which degree of passivism, just laugh and walk away, '…my self-image is not based in the mockery of the Enemy…'

Regardless of how the recipient(s) react(s), or not, there remains a 'residual imprinting' on the fields as according to Zero Point Field Theory. Thus, 13: Karma has Memory.

This either activates instantly, near-instantly, with a short delay or a long delay i.e. a Granny yells back that you are the Stupid Dumbshit but does not swing her cane… As according to Degree Of Severity, if you tried to steal her bag she swings and hits you in the head with whatever ensuing damages and court cases resulting for some time.

This is very significant. The actual mechanism of the Physic's of the different delays triggers entirely different Theory's of Karma and Reincarnation.

If it is instantaneous or near-instantaneous then it is active Energy. If it is a short or long delay then it is passive Energy.

How does this work? Thus, 14: Karma and Reincarnation is a natural mechanism which obeys a program. Let's call it Karma and Reincarnation Program of Universal Matrix.

Lynn McTaggart herself and other Scientist's with IT Specialist's do no longer deny the possibility of such a program inherent in the Universe, not just the Science Fiction Film Trilogy The Matrix, otherwise the whole of Reality only dissolves into Chaos.

The Law Of Repulsion And Attraction plays a strong role here. The problem is, how does Karma calculate through Time the Near-Infinite Variables?

2. Dependency

For Reincarnation to be true and even real, like the Resurrection of Christ in Christianity, then Karma has to be true and even real.

'Just because you do not believe in Karma does not mean it does not exist.'

GOD, Spirit, Form, Light, Shadow, Ether, Fire, Air, Water and Earth are all bound within the Host Body, Mind, Soul to different degrees, 'Son of GOD = Sun of GOD.'

It is not likely this one Lifetime is our only chance or else suffer from entering unending mass depression.

It is highly unlikely Hell and/or Heaven is forever, it just feels like forever, '…if you're put away for centuries into the Army's of Lucifer do you ever come back…'

'Debts not paid in this life are incurred in the next one…'

After all, if I cannot make it good in this one or get even in the next one, then what is the point?

'Always get even, never get angry.'

How you are born through your Genetic's and Environment has an underlying Cause. It is not completely random or GOD is a madman. You do not spring out of Nothingness or GOD has no plan.

'We are just actors on a stage.'

Does not the difference in your Pain and Pleasure come from various causal factors? Why does someone for no apparent reason get hit by a truck and land with brain damage in the hospital? Only Randomness is so absurd it results, once again, in only Chaos ruling the Universe.

With all the Battles and War's to date throughout millennia how do you know you didn't kill a thousand microscopic Enemy's…

'All things remain uncertain until…' Kaboom!

The whole framework of your Birth and taking your first step on Planet Earth is governed by previous developments, like from Darwin Ape to Neanderthaler to Homo Sapien, from Adam and Eve and the first temptation of the snake to now and into the future.

Who really was the first Human with his or her Original Sin? Can you blame an Ape for killing for food? Yet such still, regardless of your positions, causes new Timelines.

GOD cannot be Finite for then GOD would be only Mortal. Time loops. The Universe has no beginning nor end. This is a difficult concept for Bi-Polar Human to comprehend stuck in Duality. Even Islam supports most of these theories.

'There can be only one.'

'There never is only one.'

'Never say never…'

One can also cite the Platonic Universe. Is it not possible there are Virtual Ideas, Form's and Energy's which have existed, though not in Material Plane Of Existence, forever?

What do you think each one learns from youth?

'We are each just sub-programs of the mother program…'

Karma, however, cannot function with i.e. Suicide in *only* this Lifetime. Then I can just rip, steal and rape whatever and whoever I want for a million bucks, live it up for a decade and off myself when they try to catch me. That is once again Chaos full blown.

With various Types Of Karma from i.e. Buddhism, you too can experience all kinds of delights and tortures within only 75 years! Relative to the Age of the Cosmos it is starting to look like those who are Anti-Karma and Reincarnation are falling into absurdity. Our vary Solar System was formed by collisions.

3. Quantity's And Quality's

Karma functions like Time as subjective, relative and virtual Quality's on the Quantity's of Object's and Being's, in the plural and not the singular…

If that's not an equation then nothing is…

Talking about such, now we can blow all of Mathematic's away, not to mention their computer, with High Abstract Mathematic's necessary to calculate something invisible in such huge Quantity's and Quality's.

'All things are solved in Time…'

One Form has multiple Quality's. These can be any property out of ALL Element's including sensual and non-sensual. A Being and Object can be in multiple parts which are continuously changing, therefore this concept of a single part is lacking. Technically speaking you could say even GOD = ALL, not GOD = ONE, unless One Reality = GOD. Here we get many confusions in terminologies and definitions in Religion's, Philosophy's and Sciences.

We can talk here now of Sicknesses And Diseases which are not just a result of Modern Society but of your Genetic's and the choices you make in your Environment.

Due to the variables involved, which are now accelerating even more, most things are complicated and not simple. We do have about 6,6 Billion people in 2014…

Humanity will also not be able to prove Telepathy and/or Telekinesis within decades only instead of centuries, maybe not possibly until 2051 though they did make a wireless Brain-To-Computer Command in 2008 and made a 3D Monkey Puppet move.

My point is without diverging too much is that just because we haven't proven it yet doesn't mean that Karma and Reincarnation won't be proven in the near future and it is no longer solely the realm of Religion, Philosophy and/or Mysticism but Quantum Science which is discovering more and more, smaller and smaller, subtler and subtler particles and waves.

4. Event Of Reincarnation

There being multiple 'R' words here of relevance, one can plausibly put them all under the Category: Reincarnation.

Reincarnation can only happen after the Death of the Being and Object. What is rarely focused on, most claiming it is impossible, is the Death of the Spirit. Is a Spirit not just a higher Form? It then also needs to reincarnate into a different Form. That depends though where you place Spirit and Form in the hierarchy. Does not the Spirit actually stay alive and then go into another Form and then into another Mind, Heart and Body.

Here we can, once again, talk about Planes Of Existence, external and internal, also about lower and higher Forces.

No one has brought back any valid evidence or proof of the Afterlife. Why not just put it on a computer screen, '…he's dead Jim…' Until such happens no Scientist in their right mind will believe in the Afterlife, let alone practically anyone else through disillusionment.

There can be a period of Time in which you can reflect in a kind of Bardo or Limbo State, not just the Country you live in, or it can be instantaneous or near-instantaneous. You may have a choice with a Karmic Point System, your Debt's on the left column and your Credit's on the right column in a long papyrus resulting in your options. You might have no choice at all and it is automatic. Is your Spirit at all Self-Conscious, where do you go to, a big computer room with all of these dead people, the waiting line is long.

It seems fully automatic is more probable or everyone will just choose for the best possible scenario with their Credit's and damn the torpedoes.

5. Law Of Conservation Of Energy

Does this apply to both spiritual Energy and physical Energy? Spiritual Energy is in the Universe and is extra-planing, thus not outside or external to the Universe. Could I not just play GOD if my Spirit does not follow the same laws to reincarnate?

If the Universe is expanding then is there not more and more Energy available? Or was the experiment conducted in an isolated vacuum going back to the good old Classic Physic's days where pressing the gas pedal meant acceleration and not sudden impact velocity out of nowhere with StarGate Technology...

Most intuitively feel that Soul and Spirit are not limited by the Body but then, once again, a Massless Object cannot exist. If it exists it has to follow same Law's Of Universe.

This then leads again to Big Explosion and Big Implosion Theory's. If it is One Reality just getting bigger and bigger then it's adding Energy and Matter. However, the Black Hole takes away again.

It seems Law's Of Physic's cannot explain Spirit and Soul again since these could be Near-Massless.

When you die, your life has a 'sum total greater than the parts'. In any case, this is still an imaginary number of quantitative and qualitative values which not even Quantum Science can grasp unless one can stick their finger on Love and Hate.

It is therefore only highly likely that the physical Body has Conservation Of Energy but not highly unlikely that the spiritual Body has such.

So, not only in Religion, Philosophy and/or Mysticism do we have signs of Karma and Reincarnation but we do have indications in Classic Science, Quantum Science and Mathematic's, it just really is at Near-Infinite Variables.

If you have X Quantity's of Being's and Object's with their parts and Y Quality's on each of such they you have a working model to calculate Karma with Near-Infinite Variables. You also have to allow for a lot of other factors. This is near-impossible, not impossible.

It's like a big happy, neutral and unhappy X-Machine with a GOD Program, or a God-Like Monster Machine which is hopefully not out of control...

Yet, Infinity is a Constant.

Karma And Reincarnation Is At Near-Infinite Variables

Part 2 of 3

6. The Actual Unique Combination

The concept of Karma being only a quantitative phenomenon, such as only a particle, is false. One can never say it somehow does not know the difference between a dog or a tree, otherwise it does not function at all.

The more important question here is what qualities does the Being or Object possess? The second question is how does Karma know the radiance of a tree or the friendliness of a dog? The third question is about the actual functioning of Karma and Reincarnation relative to the Quantity's and Quality's which Being's and/or Object's possess.

A. Quality's

Let's take some more examples. A pack of cigarettes is loaded with about 4000 chemicals. When lit, it gains possibly even more... What lights it... where it is lit... how it is ignited... who gets ignited... and why it is exploded! Ditto for Drug's And Alchohol.

This is positive and/or neutral and/or negative. Think about just walking in there. Think of all the Money spent on the above alone and then throw in firearms, cars, busses, trams, trains and planes. Then throw your kid on Internet, too.

We now have another Type Of Karma: Collective and Individual. Types Of Karma are qualitative, not quantitative. You can see the impact.

B. How Does Karma Know?

So, how can Karma ever know this as a natural phenomenon? Does it possess Consciousness? Can it decide? Is it just a whole bunch of vessels called Stupid and/or Smart Being's and/or Object's retaliating upon each other out of simple reaction?

It is apparently rational and irrational all at the same time.

'Stupid Human is on a roller-coaster ride going straight downhill at a 95° negative learning curve and accelerating...'

If it is only a quantum number system then what is keeping count? Some say it is the zero-point-field which has a Memory System, not to mention the fine Null EM Potential, however we know that we have each a Memory, albeit mostly fuzzy. For example, it often takes years before an Investigative Officer solves a case, sometimes incorrectly, about 9 out of 10 cases are unsolved, the vast majority are with witnesses and before the advent of Internet well just get lynched by the Villager's to make sure.

Others say it is GOD. Or, is it just my God and/or Goddess through the hierarchy with Angel's and Demon's conducting unending Debates, Battles and War's upon each other. After all, since you're going to reincarnate anyway, what's a few million ants each and every year… The statistics are mind boggling on this one, some say the normal Rate Of Death per year on Planet Earth alone of only Human's is 56 million. Whatever the hell is the Rate Of Birth in comparison? After all, through specialization, they do know almost everything in a Sector. However, what is the motivation of Good, Neutral and/or Evil to transmigrate so many for in a State Of War the suffering is great by many.

This was the purpose of Mohammed to unite the tribes and why the images, statues and symbols of the Old God's were destroyed, however now in beginning of 21st Century they have once again fractured into more than a couple dozen factions. Also, the other Monotheism's stating that they can kill Immortal's is absurd, not just to Greek's, Celt's and Roman's who persist to today but to practically all other Religion's, Philosophy's and Mysticism's for the Spirit transcends and/or descends and takes another Host Body. Thus, more simply put where does a baby come from and how does it talk so soon and fast… By definition you cannot kill that which is not killable, that is a Basic Self-Contradiction in theory, belief and conviction. Maybe the clue is that the Immortal's have simply learned how to master such an ability which the vast majority of Soul's and Spirit's have not developed to yet… This reminds me of some Film's which have this as their primary Topic And Theme. About TAT, to not get too long winded, do I keep my Money And Possession's, again, into the Afterlife, well no, not according to Greek Philosophy with the River Of Styx, '…one 5 cent copper coin gets you across…'

As stated here in the previous chapter, Karma cannot *only* be some foolish Stupid and/or Smart Human taking it into his or her hands for such causes another vicious circle, '…and of all of the plans laid down by mice and men…' you could even as a Genius make a small miscalculation and Null Boom Bomb and/or another f'in vendetta.

If it is not at least analogous to a perfectly calculating computer in god-mode, allowing for some insignificant randomness, then there is no Objective Order left in Reality!

Human can do whatever the hell he/she wants and suffer the consequences which results, again, in Mass Extinction, except if everyone keeps reincarnating, except if we destroy Planet Earth before we extra-plane to Space Colony's. Will there only be a thousand survivors in the near-future, the theoretical model for survival chances…

No, rather, Human can simply not at this time comprehend such perfection in the Universe and see how microscopic we really are, but then with such sight Human would no longer be a Mortal Human anymore… I am not such, these are just my arguments.

C. Karma Functions

Let's get this clear: Whereas Smart and/or Stupid Human may dysfunction (often on purpose) the system of Karma functions.

Just like a computer system it has bugs, quarks and hacks. A 3D Game has god-mode, you can never win but really I'm still having fun… Degree Of Difficulty is erroneous.

Let us take the concept or theory of the memories of the zero-point-fields and other fields and apply it to all planes of existences. Does the cell not have a memory, does the DNA not have a memory, does the impact or a meteor on Planet Earth not spread Alien Organism's, does the death of a star not leave a residual Cause And Effect?

This is no problemo, however there is no evidence or proof as to how the Karma bites you in the ass at some undetermined time.

Is it like the theory of the scales and ranges of possibility and probability? You know, like your age and your Lifetime Expectancy.

It still has to be a near-perfect calculation with residual data left, nothing is perfect, but it is fluctuating, like again, do you stop smoking at 40, 50 or going 60 around the corner. And what you do each day does affect your Timeline, '...whatever you do, now, don't turn right on your bike with a smartphone and make a typo...'

Making an equation which can be proven with scientific models would hit the entire wall of the University. But, ya Heaven's, always leave something to the Expert's.

If I had to take a swing at it myself, not that I'm an Expert, more like at best I got a Master of the Art's with a number of Bachelor's, I'd go: A + B − C x Time = Karma Activation. Don't quote me on it though, since it could also be A − B + C / Time = Karma Activation. It could also be all real and virtual combinations of the Near-Infinite and Infinite Mathematical Equation's. It could also just be ALL Mathematical Equation's...

This, however, still does not account for qualitative values which Math cannot do.

We're after all dealing with One Reality = GOD here.

7. Karma Is Not Literal

People take things, in this day and age of rampant dominating and out-of-control Science, Technology and Materialism, though granted there are exceptions just like the 1st Renaissance by relatively a few who still claim there are some Moral's and Ethic's to hold on to, next to huge disillusionment in Religion's which don't materialize bread and conduct more War's, with Hyper Modern City's getting huger and huger, more advanced and more advanced, more complex and more complex, costing more and more and more like we all have become Near-Enlightened, way too literally. In the beginning of the 21st Century we wonder if anyone cares anymore for anything except their own agenda and how to get more and more Money while, once again, the vast majority die, starve, half-starve and go in debts. That famous American Graph put in the media proves that there really is still just a 01% Rich Elite.

'Money makes the world go Kaboom!'

The point here is, of course, Karma does not mean if I trash a whole Auto, by accident even, that a whole Auto will trash me, by accident even. We often see this in a lot of Court Cases where, '...the punishment never fits the crime...' You can also not explain away accidents as having come from accidents cause you don't know where it is originating from, that is just randomness from randomness, and in the case of a Child, you can only be prosecuted as an Adult starting at 16+ except in extreme cases, it remains inexplicable, thus there is an originating Cause And Effect playing a role even potentially from a previous Lifetime. Once again, why were you born in this Family?

It somehow gets transformed in some measure of equivalency.

Is this the Quantity's and Quality's of Positive, Neutral and/or Negative Energy's? With Energy's I mean, of course, Matter's and Energy's, Matter and Energy which are transmutable. Yet, I still don't know what my Mind is since I'm looking out two eyeballs.

How does it transfer into my computer box?

It somehow knows the equivalence to me, it is my computer box talking to me! This is now not unusual since Windows 8.0 supports Speech Recognition for Handicap's in multiple languages in 2014…

This throws Logic into Bad Scenarios, since Logic begs so much Absolutism.

Here is also the problem of the Time Delay or Delay Effect which hurls the worst Black Box Effect at everyone, '…the next day it's already heresy…' and '…can I get a witness?' Is it locking on and tracking? Is your own body, mental and spirit fields getting a little sticky? Would you please stop trying to finger me as to why I do manual encryption on folders and files…, 'If they already have access then it's too late…'

'Oops, it's that time of day, check everything near site and my computer…' Actually doing this one at 17:58, 28-07-2014 with a standard manual update I got three in a row.

My point is can one not do anything without getting some Type Of Karma, therefore stuck as according to Buddhism on the Wheel Of Life And Death, for like forever…, 'Pls don't mind, again, my Object Convention and Sense Of Humor, it's not dissin'…'

Also according to them, who are also relative, though they say Buddha reached Pure Objectivism and Nirvana, and who were the scribes in Christianity too, these cycle go on in Pralayas and Mantavaras for tens of thousands of years, apparently Planet Earth is now doomed for about 36000 years on the next cycle or so…, 'I don't plan on hanging around for that long…' This is allowed for such teaches Individual Transcendence but then they state that Buddha being the 24th Tirthankara was also the last…, now here's the catch I think for the statement ends with, *on Earth*…

Maybe we have to *not simply* transcend beyond Planet Earth like landing on the Moon.

Must one quest for a Near-Infinity for Knowledge and Experience before you gain Enlightenment and/or Immortality?

More pure even you can go with Jainism, 'The chances of you gaining enlightenment are less than a fish surfacing in the ocean in a life-saving ring…'

I am, of course, in each instance paraphrasing mildly to add accentuation and meaning. Look up on Internet what the 'literal' statements are. This is part of my point.

'Searching leads to Knowledge, leads to Power, leads to Corruption, leads to World Domination, leads to Space Colonization, leads to Galaxy's, leads to the whole Universe…'

'The individual cannot be separated from the collective.'

Does one have to shed all of one's Karma thereby killing the Ego, Self, Body, Mind and Heart just to escape with Soul and/or Spirit from Reality? No, it surely means from your present State Of Emprisonment; once again, you cannot escape from One Reality.

It could very well mean the Kingdom Of Heaven means a Soul and/or Spirit Realm where you are no longer shackled by the chains of the Body for I really do need the other ones through Correct Choice or Right Choice. However, there is also, '…my Body is my Temple…' since if you just bomb your Body with Sex, Drug's and Rock And Roll all the time, or live as a dirty pig, then you will also land there.

There is definitely some confusion here about Good, Neutral and/or Evil!

'What to you is Sin is to me Liberosity…'

8. Positive, Neutral and/or Negative Karma

It is necessary, as a basis, to simplify certain and uncertain Element's of Karma and Reincarnation. Since almost everyone is high on Hollywood, I myself am a Film Junkie having now seen thousands of Film's, Series and 3D Games…

The gray regions alone on Good, Neutral and/or Evil and Positive, Neutral and/or Negative Karma is the next equation of this essay. It, too, results in Near-Infinite Variables, 'You do not know the lines from the f'in limits!'

Any Thought, Word and/or Action carries Karmic Value. Thought weighs less than Word which weighs less than Action. These are bound to each EM Field. This is qualitative and quantitative. For example, Planet Earth has a much larger and stronger EM Field than an Individual.

One here can then argue the payoff potential of such Incomes across Expenditures, however more often than not the Profit goes straight into the short-term greed of Individual's, Corporation's and Government's who have no plan to save Humanity and/or Planet Earth.

To complicate matters it works on physical and spiritual levels in Body, Mind and Spirit which apparently the Soul is bound to. Matter/Energy/Spirit is still highly debatable since most proclaim that Matter and Energy have no Consciousness.

Consciousness, Self-Consciousness and Free Will are very important here granting Human a great amount of Power over all other Being's and Object's.

9. Moral's and Ethic's

We have so many Likes and/or Dislikes, Loves and/or Hates. We even have countless Neutral's in our little black books. We then have Need's and/or Want's. There is then the Individual and/or Collective Good and Greed.

'Do what you want as long as you harm no one.'

'A profitable enterprise has the primary purpose of attracting Noobies, not killing them…'

Does Karma really bounce back 10 times, 5 times, 2 time, or is it right on the nose 1:1?

Is there any such thing as Black Or White Scenario?

If you take a statement, out of context, and put it into the Isolated Space Complex does it only then have validity?

'You are missing the spirit in the law.'

If I kill a Woman to save a Man and the national security of a Country then what is the Greater Evil? That's fairly clear cut but what if it was just highly relative self-defense?

If I sacrifice 1 million happy bunnies for some cosmetics then Human's do not suffer is it just a question of development, progress through evolution? Or is that not Human testing or cell testing or DNA texting or Genetic's. What if they are food?

Is it really even possible to do a global case system or an individual case system?

'The mean does not exist…'

As you see the role of the Philosopher is not to only pose questions, but to reveal Truth.

Moral's And Ethic's are so relative it has become terribly weakened…

What we truly need are more clear-cut new modern adaptive Rules And Law's which do not cause all of these Cascade Effect Exception's. This can be realized with governing bodies but what happens in practice and competition is only a handful of people decide the fate of millions again, '…thanks for the eye rash anyway, asshole…'

'If you make one exception then they make exceptions to everything in the book.'

We also need to control our Logic and Emotion. Without self-control you're just an Anarchist, not even an Atheist who at least follows only the numbers. Still though, 'You are each now just a Planck Number with a chip in your palm.'

10. Karma Is Not Taking It Into Your Own Hand's

With the world in this day and age this statement should be self-evident. Yet, Human's Ego, Logic and Emotion likes to discuss, debate, intellectualize and rationalize Human's own Thought's, Word's and Action's. It gives one a cushy little happy warm wet soft spot inside to justify all of Human's deeds.

One thinks as a bipolar Human that one is doing Justice and/or Crime when one has not even memorized and cross-referenced the Rules and Law's of the Country. Unfortunately, this becomes even more absurd at cross-language and cross-culture, '…it's more like I'll stick a crossbow between your eyeballs.'

The irony of this, is no Human is capable of this. Thus, a massive Computer called GOD Computer with Jesus Email will take over the world. Yet, does this Computer not exist on only Planet Earth made by Human in a huge Universe?

'Human's ego is massively inflated.'

'The only thing inflated around here is your ego.'

'Popping someone's Ego Bubble is just plain fun.'

'Stick's and Stones *and* your Word's will definitely hurt me!'

Is Humanity with all of its crisis and victories and events itself not microscopic in Reality? Is the Individual, except a world famous Celebrity, not nanoscopic?

Yet, what you do can still affect a whole street, neighborhood, district, city, country, continent, island and/or world. Now we can affect other planets too and have very little self-responsibility as a Race or Species…

'I am the world, solar system, Universe!'

Thought's, Word's and Action's also send out ripples, waves, tides…

These cause trigger chain reactions…

This could be the key to what qualitative values are, thus the waves and not the particles which are quantitative.

By thinking as a Smart and/or Stupid Human, more or less, that you are making things even by hijacking, kidnapping, killing, murdering and/or assassinating then you have lost a major fraction of your sanity.

'Always get even, never get angry.'

'Breaking even sucks, but it's better than losing buckets.'

'Not only get even, but make a killing doing it.

Karma And Reincarnation Is At Near-Infinite Variables

Part 3 of 3

11. The Only Way To Escape Karma And Reincarnation Is To Not Exist

I technically answered this already in the previous chapter with the transcendence of the Spirit freed from the Body and other parts, however it is still a good point to focus on due to its paradoxical nature.

One has to therefore ask, are our conceptions of Real and Virtual, existing and non-existing somewhat confused? Do we not actually, in most cases, mean this Material Plane Of Existence with all its physical Law's... Very rarely does anyone use the context of entire Reality for this causes problems in axioms, beliefs and superstitions. If there is only One Reality with multiple Planes Of Existence then there actually isn't anything 'supernatural' or 'paranormal' or any of the other diverse words to describe inexplicable and/or invisible phenomena.

Human has, thank my God and Goddess, simply not discovered such Occult Secret's hidden in the fabric of Space Time. These days, anyone who claims to know such is called at best a New Age nut job, at worst locked up in an Insane Asylum.

I, myself, have had plenty of experience, not just work experience, in Mental Institutes for my own Celebrity Addiction's causing Bi-Polar Disorder, Epilepsy, Paranoia and Psychosis which are commonly misinterpreted with Psychotic Schizophrenic. For such I have taken almost every cure and pill in the book but now it's Depakine and Abilify with Thiamine so I can quit Marijuana, Cigarettes and Alchohol. However, unlike in the 60's and 70's these new drugs don't cause internal and/or external Audio and/or Visual Hallucination's which my previous Doctor wrote a book on called A Dictionary of Hallucinations by Dr. Blom. I also have 1st Year in Psychology and 2nd Year in Philosophy at York University. They do, however, cause major Neuro-Biological imbalances in your Body, Heart and Mind in Psychology or Gonads, Organ's and Brain in the case of Psychiatry. These two are also commonly confused and these days there is practically no more Freud and Jung due to the costs. Lucid Dream's I do have in plenty though if my sleep is not disturbed which is an inspiration for my Science Fiction/Fantasy books. I have now published 5 books myself. See AuthorHouse UK for my list or visit my two websites.

However, the fact remaining is that another Plane Of Existence, Alternate Reality or Dimension does not per se follow the same laws as the material one. That's almost End Debate already but, once again, where is the evidence and proof?

The classic example, the Dream World, is the Astral Plane.

Thus, the point here is not obscured, it would be much too easy and convenient to escape your Karma just by exiting this Reality i.e. Suicide. This most certainly does not save you. Quite the contrary, in fact, by definition you have unresolved Issues. These can be difficult to pry out, especially if they go back to Child Traumas where your autonomic defense mechanisms block out the memories. In some cases doing so, as in Hypnosis, causes more Psychosis and can be dangerous, so I'm really not for excessive experimentation. Buddhism also teaches the Middle Path.

All Universes, except one of Pure Chaos possibly underlying, without Order cannot exist due to total instability, therefore Karma and Reincarnation being the governing natural mechanism with conscious intervention is a Universal Truth.

'Call it what you want, I do prefer a Lotus.'

Unlike primitive pre-Modern Human System's, there are no loops and holes, except some apparent randomness, for such would lead to total self-destruction, collapse, implosion and explosion; despite the fact we see this every day in the International New's now on Planet Earth, the Solar System has been here for a long time and will still be here for a very long time.

The interesting part here is this actually lines up with Symmetry and Asymmetry in harmony and disharmony with Buddhism (and many others like Confucianism, Hinduism, Celticism etc. shown in their Art and Architecture). One can only reach Nirvana by getting off the Wheel Of Life.

Through a complex process, which the average Westerner is baffled by, you lose or gain, dissolve or build, Good and/or Neutral and/or Bad Karma. Some being born with less or more than others you can now also see the necessity of Reincarnation.

'Particles emitting waves are bound to my body and spirit…'

'Attraction and repulsion is the only universal law…'

If I can just steal from and off everyone with no consequences, do a Hail Mary, Confess or Convert on my death bed, living in Greed and Wealth for 50 years even, then wouldn't the entire Universe be insane?

It states to escape we must not exist anymore, since if you exist you cannot fail to cause more Karma, however that was before Christ, who's teachings were perverted, and there was no such thing as a computer, except manual counting Chinese racks, and the terminology and translations used have led to massive confusion about such. It actually means the difference between Life and Death, physical and spiritual Existence as to when and where you need to reincarnate. However, I can still argue the Spirit exists though not on this Material Plane Of Existence so technically you don't have to reincarnate back into a physical Body which is most likely what all the texts mean, for repeated everywhere is 'the ending of your suffering' through various means. The Spirit if it still suffers has to come back and reincarnate otherwise it is freed. But to do what, explore the Universe in Only Observation Mode, well no, Spirit does not fail, especially through Ideas to exert force over Matter, thus Spirit/Energy/Matter is theoretically not impossible, either…

After such a Near-Impossible Transcendence you evolve after your last Lifetime in a physical Mortal Coil through the higher Planes Of Existence.

12. Time Is Bound Closely With Karma And Reincarnation

Time is not only bound closely to Karma and Reincarnation, but it is inseparable. With no Time there is no need for such.

What is therefore interesting are elementary particles or universal particles, which though never die do still move through Time. See Quantum Physic's in i.e. Scientific American which

I have become a reader of. They merely change in the configuration of Form like you probably have learned in Chemistry.

REMEMBER: This material is at a min of 16+ years old equivalent you naughty one.

What is relevant here is the fascinating time released action of Karma on such a ridiculous quantity and quality of instances. I mean, just suddenly for no apparent reason some Noobie, while listening to the Voices, goes straight into 2 Trees, both horizontally and vertically, she dies in a burning ball of great incendiary release, ooh yes, finally free… not therefore.

Are we all ticking Time Bomb's?

The theories alone on this one are innumerable, so I'll go down this path… oops…

What is clear is the cyclical nature of this phenomenon, what goes around comes around.

What is also evident is it is a ranged variable. Depending on certain and uncertain Event's on the part of the Subjective Individual and the Objective World it will knock you back in the head between X Begin Time and X End Time with quantitative and qualitative values at different Delay Effect's including longer, near-instantaneous and instantaneous.

'Insta Karma gonna get ya!'

It also has a Degree Of Severity which can either lessen or heighten through Time; this being a direct ratio of whether it's resolved yet or not.

You then, after X End Time have a Release Point, like exiting Jail, where you no longer benefit or suffer from the Karma, except if you reenter the Crime Syndicate whether or not due to a poorly organized system.

'…not granting Welfare can be a Crime and leads to homelessness and more Crime.'

If you have to put a number on how long it takes in Time to no longer have any Karma from committing Murder then you have the Law Of Equivalency: However long it takes the Subjective Individual's and the Objective World, whichever is longer, to recover from the act is the equivalent quantity of Time it takes. The problem is we have no way whatsoever of quantifying all of these qualitative values. This also results in Near-Infinite Variables of Karma and Reincarnation.

This can, of course, also be a positive Force, like a Golden or Silver Age.

If you perceive Karma only at a simplistic level of different combinations of plus and minus Credit's in different Bank Account's which are fluctuating through Time then you get a better Idea, but what plays in the background is a Spiral Vortex, a Circle Loop and a Sphere Spin.

'Until the beginning of the 20th Century, America did not have any National Debt!'

The problem for the Scientist is no different than the difference between Classical Empirical Science and Modern Quantum Science.

To put these charts, and even to measure them in Human's, would require super quantum devices, for Karma is simply more subtle and smaller than quantum particles and waves. Is Time the most subtle of them all?

Or, Karma is the purely virtual functioning, through even Mathematic's, of all the particles and waves.

However, we keep trying to quantify everything when there is Spirit in Death.

13. Karma Has Photogenic Memory

The most outstanding theory for this is Zero Point Field Theory which as one of its quantities and/or qualities is able to store the entire History of the Universe.

It makes sense that we leave imprints and residual Energy's. If I hit a table it does not disappear and it hits back, hard enough and it hurts. Also, if it is just one big mindless now here continuum with no record then, once again, Reality, 'Universe please don't go away…' and everything is reduced to ludicrous Nihilism.

Somewhere it has to be stored. All levels of Life show different Degrees Of Memory; even birds know where to migrate to each year.

More important even, cells and genes know how to regenerate.

'History repeats itself, unending…'

It is not so hard to believe how Karma of Culture, Race and/or Species comes back, but how does the Universe keep track of the entire Planet or even Solar System?

This, too, can only be an automatic natural mechanism. The idea of GOD or SATAN keeping a diary on each and everyone is absurd unless it is automated.

When Genetic's is more fully understood in the next 20 years then we will have a better understanding of how Memory works…

'The Macrocosm reflects the Microcosm, no, only the Microcosm reflects the larger Macrocosm cause it cannot exert enough Force.'

The best answer so far is imprinting; when we repeat the learning material, a different quantity of times by different Relative IQ Level's it grows a stronger line in our brain.

A couple other cute analogies are the Arkasic Record's, Library's of the Universe ad infinitum a Mainframe Database.

Who would be writing it all, Universal Bard's?

'And the bard is still sitting at the side of the battlefield rapidly writing it all down, his words and pen in flame…'

Information, such as person's names, are bound to Object's. How could the Universe know all the names if it was Emanual Kant I Do It Again?

Only a massive Computer, including visuals, could possess all this data. Such a natural Computer with unlimited Memory, therefore, has to exist in Reality, for otherwise there is nothing left of any History. And when our Sun goes Super-Nova will there be anything left of our History?

14. Karma And Reincarnation Program Of The Universal Matrix

In the same line, if you take, like the Film Trilogy, The Matrix, the entirety of our Reality as one big Computer analogy then all Being's and Object's can be perceived as different programs.

There are in complexity different combinations of Matter/Energy/Information/Spirit which sounds more like the correct order.

Of course, the once catch in this argument is that there is to date, and by definition, no such thing as an ensouled Self-Conscious AIL.=^|=ArtificialIntelligentLifeform.¡! =duhrobot=Psibog=”Hi!I’mnotactuallybiological, so how can it be the same??!”

If you take the analogy as far as being part of a whole whose functioning is governed by Rules and Law’s then fine, but then you throw in Free Will and it all goes to Hell again!

If I am just a program then where’s the Privacy Protocol Port, the 14 Law’s of Karma and Reincarnation, although I’m sure I missed a couple like the Chakras which everyone talks about and energized cells, preventing me from dropping that piece of shit computer off a 32 Story Building?

O.k. an ‘A’ for Science and Mathematic’s, but then the axioms change or have no validity in another smaller plane of existence, dimension, reality.

One can never control the immitigable Spirit and Soul who will always quest on for Freedom and Peace.

‘You can bring a horse to the firewater but you can’t make it drink.’

Whereas inanimate, though the term is almost antiquated, Object’s may be ruled by such Law’s, the Being’s follow other Rules!

This, however, does not throw everything back into Chaos, as those freaks cheer for, ‘I’m a freeeeeeak tooo…’ so that’s no Insult.

Fortunately, the vast majority of Being’s are extremely microscopic and limited in Power And Energy = Force.

GOD only knows what would happen if my own High Wizard went haywire…

Some Possible Theories

Below are some possible theories which I have been contemplating. If there is an answer to anyone of them soon, let's say in a decade or so, is highly debatable

1. The Sentient Computer

Example PHP code:

```php
<?php
$My_Spawn = new CC_Spawn('Silver, High Wizard');
echo $My_Spawn->get_CC();

class CC_Spawn {
private $CC;
public function __construct($content) {
$this->CC = $content;}
public function get_CC() {
return $this->CC;}
}
?>
```

$this tells the whole class what CC is. It is available to all functions. This starts with __ construct function. It transfers 'Silver, High Wizard' in $content through the built in __construct function of PHP. This is then passed to get_CC method through $CC property. It actually works backwards going back to the top of the script.

Private is only in class and public is extra-planar of class, thus global.

Can a computer become Self-Conscious? If you refer to contents of another folder through its path then the computer can cross-reference.

The tentative answer is 'yes', in fact with all of the knowledge on Internet a Super Computer can become Super Sentient.

The question, of course, remains can the Soul or Spirit ever occupy such an artificial mechanical body and possess Free Will through randomness like a Human can or will it just be highly complex knowing numbers and words only.

The tentative answer is 'no', only a living Spirit can enter a living Being. Also the randomness would still be artificial, not truly having Free Will. Free Will needs intent.

Intent is very important to do something since I simply choose whenever I want to go and get a hamburger, cola and fries. The only way a Computer can do this is if someone types in an agenda…

2. The Null Theory

The Null Theory at first sounds incorrect. How can something which does not exist affect Reality and the Universe? Or even how can Nothing itself have influence? Think about Null Potential hand in hand with Kinetic Energy. If you drop a ball from a great height it can wipe out a city. Though this is, of course EM Gravity, Potential Energy is a scientific fact.

Also, Nature abhors a vacuum… The Null Theory can explain all of the motion in the Universe for all things trying to fill the empty space/void. This is in no way confused with Nothingness = Ether. Now, again, the Zero Point Field state there can never be 'nothing' or 'empty space' in the Universe, however such instances state nothing of what is outside of the Universe… It also does not allow what is *not* actually underlying the greater Reality and the Universe itself.

The beauty of The Null Theory is the Infinite Null Potential of Energy it can provide… The quantity of Potential Energy of Absolute Nothing, the opposite of Everything, is Infinite. Many forget that Everything has to have an opposite which is Nothing. Otherwise, Everything also does not exist!

You apparently do not believe in Eastern Theory's. To respond in one sentence: If Everything is not moving through Nothing then would not the actual friction of all the underlying and greater EM Field's burn everything up…

To pose another question, how else do you allow for an Infinite Universe if there is no Infinite Energy?

The concept of an Infinite Universe cannot be allowed without Infinite Energy. There are few theories which allow for Infinite Energy. When you look at Mathematic's, you see it still amounts to mostly Finite or Near-Infinite with i.e. exceptions of ∞, Pi, .333333… and .666666… The vast majority is used for other limited calculations and when you try to throw Infinity into equations it results in more Infinity which is no proof. Such is a poor excuse for Mathematician's and/or Computer's who cannot calculate such and then discard it too quickly has having no validity.

I would like to strengthen my argument of The Null Theory with the following points:

Empty Round Container: To fill something it has to first be empty, this is applicable at all levels of densities. The expanding spherical Universe must first be empty.

Expansion Of Universe: If the Universe is expanding then it is Near-Infinite. If it is not expanding into Nothing, which allows for Infinity, then it would burn up due to friction. What is it expanding into? Or is it just one large Infinite Reality not expanding? Of course, Finite and Near-Infinite Universe within this could be contracting and expanding.

Opposite Of Everything: Only Nothing can be opposite of Everything. We have to define things by their opposites or they do not exist. You cannot say there is only ∞ without its opposite 0. If you remember in Antiquity there was no number 0 in Mathematic's! A lot of the bias of the West is still based in such.

Null Infinite Potential: If there is Nothing outside of the Universe, which Zero Point Field Theory is obtuse about since no one can perceive it, then the Universe and/or Everything could be trying to fill it… Nothing pulling plus the Big Bang pushing would lead to acceleration. An explosion by itself does not cause acceleration.

Nothing allows for faster than Speed Of Light Travel. Light / Time with Mass as in Einstein's equation would have very little bearing since he states Light is the medium. You are not limited by the medium if it is Nothing, 'Nothing is instantaneous.' Information itself with KB's, MB's and GB's has mass, now all you have to worry about is the Light Medium. If we are limited by the medium of Light, it would take forever to explore the Universe, Galaxy and even Solar System. Even relatively nearby would take hundreds of years. Mediums are a question of the size and density of particles and waves, or in other words how 'thin' and 'light' they are… Quantum entanglement states are already showing signs of not being limited by the Speed Of Light, though this is not proven for how can two particles at any distance affect each other with no noticeable delay? The general idea here is that there is some type of door/portal/gate/hole in Space. This leads to another hole in Space Time. There are therefore holes everywhere in Space… sry, bad joke… no, such connects somehow to different coordinates. This cannot be limited by Speed Of Light, otherwise you will never get there in a very long time, let alone send a huge Space Ship. So, we are still looking for this medium and whichever Scientist and/or Mathematician can prove it will be the next greatest Einstein.

Black Hole Balance: There is also Speed Of Shadow through the Shadow Medium which could be even more subtler than Ether like the still yet unclassified dark particle as according to a Scientific American article. Black Holes could also have come into being to balance out the rampant expansion which could also tear apart the Universe and prevent or cause cannibal Galaxy's from colliding and consuming each other.

Need For EM Gravity: What greater need is there for gravity, not just speed? Otherwise, your car flies off into space, into Nothingness… Why else are things in cyclical orbital planar motion, except Object's which are too small, light and/or fast to be pulled into EM Gravity? Reality is one big balanced interacting whole of various turning mechanisms at all levels.

Infinite Equations: How else can there be unlimited or Infinite Equations equaling 0? For example, $X - X = 0$. I know, pretty lame of me, but no one can deny this simplest and oldest equation of them all.

You, once transformed from Matter to Energy to Information to Spirit (to Soul even?), connect any 2 points with coordinates with each other at any distance and any plane with 0 Mass equivalence through Nothing. This is not limited by Speed Of Light.

As an addition it would be appreciated if there are not mildly insulting and immature remarks like it is a 'null hypothesis'.

I, however, don't deny this would take a long time to prove, allowing for acceleration of learning curve, next to the off-the-scale requirements to test it.

It is also highly doubtful whether such enters the Realm Of Spirit.

3. Quantum Teleportation Is At 90 Degrees

This may also, at first, sound fat out or wrong but please be open-minded.

Quantum particles, apparently, go back and forth between a Vertical and Horizontal state perpendicular to each other. Through various steps there seems to be a way of transferring Information since you can read the on/out, right/left/, 1/0 states and therefore encode Information.

No one knows why this is, except for the combinations, and it is very unpredictable.

Well, could it not have something to do with EM and/or Gravity Field's which require Energy to come to Balance, to rest, to equal and to equilibrium. If you look at the buildings and all other Object's on Planet Earth, you see they are all standing perpendicular! The actual Forces pulling down on a building or any Object need to balance out or it will topple. One of the interesting things about Modern Architecture, though god ugly, is their usage of this Law.

Now, is it not the same Law and Force which is affecting the Vertical and Horizontal states of quanta? If you look a little further into Maxwell's Electro-Magnetic Gravitational Theory's you will see more evidence of this 90 Degree Phenomena. Not only Right Hand Thumb Rule confirms such but interacting EM Field's = EM Spheres shows it, too.

Laser emissions are also caused by the need and/or desire of particles to come to rest, in lower more stable orbits.

The right-angled triangle of Pythagoras also backs it up.

Each and everything which is interacting needs to achieve some form of balance in energies. It seems that 90 degrees is in many cases the best way to achieve this.

However, once again, it would require a Genius Scientist, which I most certainly am not, to show how such is and prove it.

It's called Quantum Entanglement too. Apparently, it allows for near-instantaneous and instantaneous teleportation.

There, however, with Time has to be some small delay…

So, let's get something straight though, therefore…

4. Telepathy Is Not Illogical And/Or Impossible

To start, it is nice to see the conversation has been engaged without too much bashing going on…

To state the brain does not actually emit Delta, Theta, Alpha, Mu, Beta, Gamma waves (and probably even other ones) through the Ether just like sounds, radio and microwave is saying your head is stuck in the isolated void of space with no interaction with the outside world; there is always the internal and external.

The experiments to date are not valid, full of holes, poorly controlled and can all be easily sabotaged by 'Hi! I'm still at Radiohead…!' This is inspired by Dr. Praag from Utrecht University in Netherlands.

There is no problem with most of your statements such as noise, distortion and what I think you mean to be dis-interference, the cancelling and/or absorption of a signal. Just because Human's brain is a dim light with a lower signal strength does not deny the possibility of Telepathy.

Also, Human has not fully developed the receptors in the brain, though there is study being done on this… See primarily, Utrecht University, Netherlands.

I would like to strengthen my argument with, actually, interference and projection. Take a moving fan, for example, if you aim a vibration at it then you can even make it talk…, 'Hellooozzzz allsss youzzzzz noobiessss outsss theressss…' Now, ok… take the same idea and apply it waves. If your ears can pick up vibrations which are then translated by the brain then there is no reason with the correct receptor in your brain that you will not actually be able to communicate via Telepathy… though, if Human developed it now then everyone would go insane…

Now, what you have, just like all the Radios, TV's, Phones, Mobiles and Computer's is the need for AMPLIFICATION of the signal to make it audible. How do you know that the Noobie's Brain is not working at 14Hz only?

So, when you combine the correct receptors with amplification of the signals/brainwaves of the Human Brain then you will be able to hear and project human thought.

Joke: There is a bwoo-tooth in my bwain and butthole… Where do you want yours?

And, even better, the only way the whitecoats will ever believe it, you will be able to show and play your thoughts on a computer screen…

On the other hand, also somewhat frightening, nothing has stopped the progress of Science into a post-apocalyptic horror science fiction film before anyway…

5. Real Unique ID

A. Security Of Passwords Ports And Protocols

What they say, especially with spying, is that there is no such thing as a Secure Password, in 2008 even Bill Gates said, 'Passwords are dead.' And what is the average lifetime of Noobie's password? On the other hand, a hardware Firewall, regular updates and a VPN with PPTP is not so bad, though not so perfect when there update delays.

What computer, networks and websites need to do is use a Real Unique ID solution. With this one does not even need a password and can use your Real Name and Real Address and Real Smartphone and Real Number with your IP Adress. Unfortunately, broadband connections which do not have their own IP Adress fail here too since they are not unique just like many names in contact forms…

'Oh sry, I meant 2695 Nick Names and 6158 usernames and passwords on Internet and countin'!' says Revlis, Vampire Demon.

We need to generate out of a set of variables a Real Unique ID for ourselves and apply it to our computers for both local and remote. We also need better authentication methods, not just with your email, such as with your Smartphone, since even if you stick a string on it that even backdoors across all the wiretapping going on. Here in the next one, you see the extent to which Government's and Corporation's aren't willing…

B. Privacy Of Public And Private Life

The payoff between Privacy and Security is still a highly debated issue. If I may do a synopsis of the Timeline as written by Esther Dyson in a Scientific American article from September 2008:

1600's: The clergy cast an ever widening net for information about civic affairs and under Puritan rule it is a civic duty to keep an eye on your neighbor.

1700's: Little privacy exists within families, they often share beds. English and Roman's concur that 'a man's house is his castle'. Mail is routinely opened.

1787: U.S. Constitution stipulates that a census must be conducted once a decade.

1791: The Bill of Rights protects freedom of speech and unreasonable searches.

1800's: The 'penny press' publishes unbridled gossip about celebrities.

1838: The telegraph is introduced and is bugged.

1890: Samuel D. Warren, Jr., and Louis D. Brandeis argue for right of Privacy.

1900: Fingerprints are established as unique.

1928: The U.S. Supreme Court legalizes seizure of electronic conversations.

1936: Social Security numbers are assigned with 9-numbers, 'You're now a Planck number' for 'most' Americans on a piece of paper.

1966: Freedom Of Information Act (FOIA) is passed.

1968: The Omnibus Crime Control and Safe Street Act, Title III specifies when a warrant is required for wiretapping, some call it 'end of privacy'.

1973: 'There is growing concern… computers… a dangerous threat to… privacy.' Horst Feistel in Scientific American article, May 1973.

1976: Whitfield Diffie and Martin E. Hellman invent public-key encryption.

1978-1994: Congress passes refinements to the wiretapping laws to be 'wiretap-ready'.

1980's: DNA, fingerprinting and cellular telephones become commonplace.

1989: World Wide Web (WWW) service is added to Intra- and Internet.

1995: The term 'spyware' is used for the first time (Windows 95 also introduced).

2001: The USA PATRIOT Act grants authorities broad discretion to search databases and conduct surveillance (on anyone).

2004: Facebook, the popular social-networking website makes its debut.

2008: Congress updates the 1978 wiretapping law, expanding the surveillance.

C. Hardware ID And Real Member ID

Real Unique ID does not mean one little replaceable chip on your motherboard, that is actually the whole problem with no latest version of firmware allowing them to simply watch what you type in and if you have a webcam, like the recent Issues in International New's then forget it, they're looking at your whole living room and no, once again, that is not the whole meaning of The Free Show. The Free Show means primarily and mostly all the Open Source on Internet.

It means the whole computer and *all* of its parts. Now is this Security or Privacy? Or is this Functionality Security Privacy? It then knows your Real Identity + Real Unique ID = Functionality Security Privacy.

Whoever *and* whatever you logon to reads this in the registration and authentication process which is automatic and no one else under your Real Unique Credential's can logon to your account. This avoids a lot of other Identity Problem's and IT Problem's which is making Internet a chaotic dysfunctional user-unfriendly unstable environment prone to anarchistic Hacker's and other Criminal's in Maffias and especially the very not unreal Enemy within the borders.

So far in 2014 we have steps by Google and Microsoft and others to provide, as an option, or non-optional, Smartphone Authentication. This helps a lot the Individual but your naughty little sister or brother who you bashed on the head too often can just grab it out of your bedroom.

Also, if your computer becomes the tool of authentication then all you have to do is turn it on like a Smartphone so he/she/it could just walk in and zombie it if there are no updates.

In addition, if there are still usernames and passwords at millions of websites then how would they react? In my own experiences with people and computer clients which extends all the way from NT to now in Win 8.1 as a Microsoft Certified System's Engineer and Webdeveloper I see that Standard User's and/or Noobies all freak out if they have to change their 'fluffy-wuffy' username and password.

Is this even applicable to WWW, do we not need WWW2, though I still find it hard to swallow typing in 'www2' or 'wwww' the whole time… it's also not intuitive to type in only after 'http' without any 'www' unless you use a search engine.

Of course, hand in hand with Real Unique ID is Real Member ID which is not a fake alias and allows you to do a lot of illegal things such as all the FREE Enertainment in the world without paying a cent and causing downfall of Modern Western Civilization again…

It depends what is Unique ID… there are a million John Smith's and a million prefabricated systems, however there are not a million Real Addresses and Real IP Addresses and Real Birth Dates and Real Social Security Number's which are the same. You can, therefore, combine many Object's and Values with each other to generate a Unique Combination.

I still have my keys and my bank card in my hands so you could stick it on a Real ID Card and please, once again, not a chip in my palm to pay twice by accident again.

D. Weakening Of System

With the quantity and quality of hacking going on these days, you can see it too with the daily updates needed and the holes in firewalls with the extreme differences between default settings, manual configurations and automatic ones, one cannot agree anymore with the weak anonymity argument which is a Major Loop in the Privacy Act pertaining to International Information Technology Law's.

Also, seen from a technical side, the ridiculous stupefying increase in weak usernames and passwords and them not being updated regularly, necessary to use practically *all* websites now, weakens the entire system.

What the Noobie, of course, does is use the same username and password for all 500 accounts… And then it's in very many instances in businesses, something easy to remember, like my bad jokes about passwords, and how about the year Napoleon was defeated by Waterloo and, you might not have heard this one, the year he sold Louisiana to finance his war against Russia…

We need badly, especially in 2014 with expected growth of Internet to tenfold in the near future an automatic solution and not all this clumsy Emanual Kant Labor thus, if possible, Fully Automatic For The People.

In any case, it will take a long time before there is any transition. If you thought trying to step over to Hybrid Car's is difficult then think of the now Huge IT World.

6. There Are Some Holes In The Black Hole Theory

It is practically impossible that a Black Hole is a Portal to another Dimension/Plane/Universe or it does not matter where, Heaven and/or Hell… Everything which has Form is destroyed and there only remains pure condensed Matter/Energy, a very large amount in a relatively small cubical space.

The best theory to date are various Universes in the Multiverse Theory which exchange Energy with each other to maintain some form of balance… but you and me and everything pulled towards it are effectively killed. The only remaining possibility, which is quite worthless, is your Spirit with no material Form, therefore pure Spirit Energy can go through. But, oh well, no one can bring back evidence from the After Life.

Response by user in a science forum on Internet (with small edits):

'Even if Einstein-Rosen bridges exist (non-traversable wormholes, then just because an astronaut unfortunate enough to fall in will be killed is no physical argument against the existence of black holes. Both the tidal forces and the high level of radiation are expected not to be healthy.

Open problems with black holes include;

The classical singularity. Do quantum effects regulate this?

When a black hole evaporates via Hawking radiation is there some kind of remnant or does it completely evaporate? What happens to the information of the material that fell in?

How valid is the no hair theorem? That is can black holes really only be classified by their mass, electric charge and angular momentum? Counter examples in higher dimensions are known.

Are all singularities out of sight behind event horizons? The cosmic censorship hypothesis says they are always hidden.

Then there are plenty of questions about super-symmetric black holes, black rings and how these are important in string theory.

Some of these really require some knowledge of quantum gravity. You should view black holes as a theoretical probe into quantum gravity.'

My response (with edits here):

'First, even Hawkings played it safe by saying 'it is not impossible that something can go through a black hole…' (paraphrase). The general idea is that something goes through and/or comes through Black Holes. Two Dutch Scientist's even read radio waves coming from one… The question is: What can go through Black Holes? Is it even possible to find this out, since anything you send to one gets severely compressed, ripped apart and then blown into another Universe or back into our own Galaxy.

Second, to reply to the complex scientific statements:

1) Singularity being the infinite density and quantum effects regulating the smaller particles, basically my response would be two things: A. Anything possessing Form and Mass and Matter would be stripped to pure Energy. B. Only the smallest particles would go through the Black Hole, therefore smaller than quanta not yet measurable by Science.

2) Hawking's radiation allowing for the dissipation of a Black Hole. In a Universe continuously contracting and expanding with continual interchange of Matter/Energy it is not impossible, of course, for a Black Hole under the right conditions to get smaller. It seems, however, it only grows, for what Force would reverse the process. Well, the release of particles. It is, however, also definitely possible that Black Holes will all grow, with cannibal Galaxy's, consume the entire Universe and at critical mass cause another Big Bang. See primordial Black Holes.

3) 'Hair' meaning all other qualities. As to higher dimensions, I prefer the words planes or worlds or realities or universes so as to prevent confusion between X,Y, Z… indeed, though, in a higher plane or different reality where different laws abide, and only if Black Holes access such, would not be limited by only mass, electrical charge and angular momentum which has the taste of Classical Empirical Science. The problem still remains you cannot just simply send a deep space probe…

4) It is leaning towards the idea, like trying to scan the core of the Sun, we can never return from such, unless, of course, a Black Hole is two way which is not impossible… also, once again, how does anyone survive the event?

7. Conclusion

I hope you, the reader, takes everything with a grain of sand, a pound of salt, and open mind and an attempt to achieve more Objectivity instead of just the whims and wills of Subjectivity, which we each suffer from in discussion and/or debate. Like I said at the beginning of this essay, these are some possibilities, theories and like with the last example with practically no evidence or proof.

'Start the debates! And don't party too much…' says Mr. Newbie, Rules Lawyer Null EM Dragon Metal Head.

The Free Society

'Money is the root of all Evil today.'

'Knowledge is free to all Humanity.'

'A Gift of God must be shared with all.'

The idea of a Free Society is a long-term utopian Society proposition which does not concern itself with the temporary biases and barriers which shall be put in its place, it will even fully circumvent these if need be.

The key or clue to this concept, the Holy Grail of Society, so to speak, is in the incentive and motivation provided to the people.

The failure of Communism is through its lack of incentive and motivation. This still leads to multiple revolutions by suppressed and repressed people.

The failure of Capitalism is through its top heavy hierarchy. As shown to us in the beginning of the 21st Century it led to recessions, massive State Debt, instability and out-of-control competition.

'A donkey with a carrot in front of its nose will walk through the entire desert.'

'At some point the donkey gets its carrot, it then wants a bigger carrot shoved all the way up its…'

'Though, Pavlov's Dog has a fine retort to this, you can train all types of Animal's to do things, they will not do such without an Award…'

'A Psychologist at the beginning of the 20th Century already studied and described, with a huge model, the Rat and Mouse Complex. Each had one small room. They even started eating each other, going completely Insane.'

As long as you give the people the incentive and motivation to keep working, to keep going, to keep fighting then they will grow.

There is so much to talk about how the Credit System will replace the Money System. This will also help stop Black Money.

In the future, according to many Film's and Series your whole life with Information Technology, and a misused Credit System, can be deleted with a single button.

Yet, what is the difference between a Point System, Credit System or Money System and who decides what the points are?

'A cleaning lady gets to earn 10 Credit's per hour.'

'A dinner costs 15 Credit's.'

Your Government who you voted for gets to decide such. Your Corporation at the website who you have a subscription at gets to decide such. Your Individual boss who you work for gets to decide such. Where are the standards?? It's all arbitrary…

Do you still trust your Government who you vote on once in the 3-5 years?

The MySQL database of 2008 does not have a single Democracy listed. You, in fact, are a Republic, Monarchy, Constitutional Monarchy, Federation, Confederation, Dictatorship, Fascism, Communism or some other form of temporary ruling Party, somewhat voted in by the people. I say, somewhat due to corruption and in NL local elections in 2013 only 50% actually voted! There was also a limited choice of Party's so I didn't bother either, so much for Socialism and/or Social Democracy too.

So, how does one ever achieve a Free Society? Not that I'm saying this should be its name, see previous essay Free Democracy in Evolutionary Essays – Part 01 – Published by AuthorHouse UK.

If I want a piece of chicken I need to give something in return. And we still hear all these jokes about the Barter System, like 50% of Europe Market is a Black Market, but there are also strong values here between i.e. Parent and Child.

'I can still give a gift.'

'It takes two to make a thing go right.'

Let us propose a new Education System where most of the mistakes come from.

'The post Hyvescool Rift is a 2 km wide canyon you have to fly over while being shot at.'

You take the Individual's, starting at a Child, environmental conditioning and genetics into consideration. You then give Test's to ascertain the Child's, Young Teenager's, Teenager's, Young Adult's, Adult's abilities, thus Talent's And Skill's.

You then decide where this Adult is best placed in The Free Society.

One difference here: You then give the Adult the Right Of Choice by his and/or her Free Will to take a Job out of the List Of Most Favorable Choices. Unemployment or Welfare or any reason means less Credit's, not that I'm going to draw a ratio with the Cleaning Lady here since it depends on your unemployment but you could say Welfare = 10 Credit's per hour only as a starting base using the decimal system rather than fully arbitrary Class Bashing.

'You cannot turn a butcher into a baker cause then you get blood pies…'

This way we *can* avoid extreme communistic, fascist, capitalistic, and if I may say so, democratic enslavement of the population at each level, since I'm not the only one saying that Democracy looks more like these days to be Welfare State Democracy.

'An Army of *no* Volunteer's is useless to me.'

'Those who do not fight for their own Free Will are useless.'

So, who pays you how much for what?

Whereas, the present Credit System is lacking and is no different from the Money System with all its capital, loans and investments, in so many ways no one can deny the Number System, thus as stated at least based on the decimal system.

'If someone wants to, or needs to, live on only 500 Credit's per month, then let 'em!'

If one can make a comprehensive Person Profile, with all of his and/or her abilities, thus Talent's And Skill's, then one can make a Number System for the Individual Animal, Human and/or Alien.

One Individual can then lead a happy productive Life, allowing for Sickness And Disease, and contribute to the welfare and profit of The Free Society.

'We want to occupy the entire Universe even.'

'Humanity will know the stars.'

How can this be done without a Number System in The Free Society?

How can this be done without the Elite Spaceship?

How can this be done without Member's of The Free Society?

How can this be done without the abilities, thus Talent's And Skill's, of all the Individual Animal's, Human's and/or Alien's?

'You, after all, are just each a number.'

As just stated, the Number System in The Free Society as part of Free Democracy does not deny the Free Choice of the Individual by Free Will leading to necessary Chaos in all systems.

'There is no Order without Chaos.'

This allows for adaptation and Evolution.

After all, if by your Right Of Choice you want and/or need to live in Poverty with no material goods then let your acquisition be at only 500 Credit's, but this cannot be 0 since otherwise you enter another Black Market Barter System.

We need to define a correct Social and Credit System to apply to the handicapped.

Does a blind Man and/or Woman deserve 1500 or 2000 Credit's in the Number System of The Free Society?

When does your heart die and deprecate at this fuckin' Money System?

It is outdated and antiquated, your books are even dated back to the 17th Century or so. Does such have any application in the 21st Century?

'If I had to write my shit on hemp instead of teak, I'd still be smokin' it!'

You can still be defined as a Sum Total of your Talent's And Skill's, though you are of course greater than the parts only continuously adapting and evolving…

You, therefore, based on your Point System within the Number System get a Total plus your Free Will. For example: English: 97%, Math: 69%, PR: 84%, IT: 61%. What now, Noobie, forget your choices in IT, yet the Total is: 301% / 4 = 75.5% which is pretty good. What do you choose with your Free Will: PR. This is, of course, a simplistic example of your Free Choice in The Free Society.

You are then assigned a Job in that Sector, if there are none then you have to choose something else. Most people will probably have many more to choose from in the future but that is realistic.

What if you just choose to specialize in IT Robotic's and get 87% while the other Candidate gets 88%? That's what you use the Total for since I've never seen, except a Robot itself who has only 1 Skill And Talent. That is even a Stupid Bot who cannot make error corrections like placing cans on a conveyor belt.

No system is perfect but at least the Number System of The Free Society provides a good basis in the decimal system and can be used as a Guideline, not a Guide or Leader or Warlord who with a sweep of his and/or her hand dismisses all again.

'For the Good and not the Evil.', 'Chaos will rule in the end.', 'It all began in Fire and it will all end in Fire…', 'Before the Light there was Shadow.', 'In the beginning there was only Nothingness', '…and throughout Everything is Nothing'.

Think And Build Vertically

Think alone of all the problems on the entire Planet which can be solved by thinking and building vertically.

With the growing population and the lack of ground thinking and building horizontally is already outdated in the beginning of the 21ˢᵗ Century.

Following are some examples of what problems, even major problems, which can be solved:

1. Fila's

Next to, of course, the idiocy of all travelling in the same direction at the same time, which is more of a necessity than just sheer ludicrous, you can probably solve the Fila Problem by thinking and building vertically.

I'm not talking about the massive infrastructures in America which simply generate more routes.

If you have a stretch of highway between two City's, 50 to 100 km long, and due to various Bottleneck Problem's there are 250+ km Fila's causing major stress and pollution you can build vertically.

Simply add a second highway on top of the first one! Just like in the past with autos and planes, it sounds ridiculous and could be God Ugly but look at where those two inventions got us; you could always add a lot of trees on both sides and in the middle to make it more aesthetically pleasing.

Technically seen, it's not even so difficult to build.

Here you already have 50% of the traffic.

In City's themselves you can do this with clean soundless public transport viaducts: 3 trains on top of each other!

Add some color and it may not, after all, be so god ugly… if you look at American City's these days then it can't get any worse for the eye, either.

2. Food Production

Have you ever wondered why there is so much empty flat land outside City's with cows and sheep and all Smart and/or Stupid Human's live on top of each other in City's? What a waste of land!

Well, how about Animal Appartment's?

Now, we have the cow, a very happy cow with healthy meat in a living room.

You can include music, TV, a window with a view and relatives. And I am most certainly not talking about those awful torture Cancer inducing Chicken Factory's… In approximately a 4 x 6 x 4 meter living room with such luxuries in a perfectly controlled environment kept clean and maintained by Modern Technology and Human Laborer's you can grow even the best organic cows. The smaller the domesticated Animal the easier it is.

You can even experiment with different Types Of Music. This meat was made with Classical, Dance, Techno, Metal and/or Hip Hop.

No activist has any counter argument here either since they can be taken out for regular walks, showers and sexual intercourse. You could even install a walking track around the pens in case it's bad weather.

In addition, if you have an Animal Appartment at the edge of the City which is i.e. 32 x by 32x in width and height you will have a massive price reduction, resource reduction and profit increase.

Now think of how many Greenhouse plants and drink you can grow…

Thinking and building vertically increases your health and happiness.

3. Living Space

People who talk about extra expensive luxurious low-rise Human Appartment's are just plain backwards: This has no realistic practical application in City's of the 21st Century. With continual immigration and increase of population the need for housing is only growing exponentially. How about a 60 Billion Population in the 22nd Century?

With this statistical trend due to increase in welfare, peace and prosperity concerns are still very erroneously building only 3-5 stories Luxury Appartment's!

There is practically no denial of the possibility of a cement complex of buildings in America from West to East coast… This increases the need for a far greater integration of Nature and Technology. Take, for example, a sky shot of an American City as seen in many Film's. Try to zoom in and find the one remaining tree… Where is it, nowhere on those streets, just one central park area with lots of smog.

So, we're better off not denying the inevitable construction and growth of the Human Population and take preventative and curative measures.

It's not even original: How about a park on top of the building with Laser Turret's…

Just don't go when it's too windy… Wahhhhhh…

There are many ways to counteract standard 'ugly' criticisms with such aesthetic improvements. Instead of just SQUARE buildings try round off tops, polyforms, colors and other Hyper Modern Technology's and Material's.

We will then even have Science Fiction like 20-50 stories Human Appartment's.

This also reduces costs, eventually, and does not lead to, with sufficient insulation, the primitive outdated post WWII rat and mouse complex.

4. Space Ship's

If this is not the epitomical example of thinking and building vertically than nothing is.

What the joke is, of course, in the late 20th Century and early 21st Century first and second generation spacecraft barely have enough room to crawl through horizontally.

Now, ok, no harsh criticism but it reminds me of 8-bit computer games.

So, as a proposition, is not our whole Evolution even going vertical…

Picture now 50 decks with 500 modules each in a large circle twirling through Space bringing the first Colonist's to another Solar System.

Well, the same can be done on Mars in the near future.

Please do not build a 1 story curvy low lying complex as depicted by many Scientist's and Artist's… Try 20 stories!!

If you can insulate each module the same way then what is the difference?

The answer is real estate.

By the same trend, looking into the far future, Mars will also fill up…

'Spread your seeds upon the earth…' so it was written. Such can be symbolic, like ants, of the propagation of Human Species into the Universe. It's definitely NOT 2D.

5. Think Up Your Own

You, too, can think and build vertically, this generates similar results as thinking laterally or Out Of The Box.

Who know, maybe you will be the one who builds it too…

Polaris

Polaris is a country of people. Being such it deserves to have its own identity. This must come primarily from the people. After all, they are what make it work.

Our present situation in Polaris, a theoretical model, is quite archaic. As a whole we are sludgy and unorganized. The Government, Corporation's, the Royal Family's, Elite Individual's and the People are in conflict with each other. They are unlikely to change their disagreeable ways.

It is imperative for Polaris to progress towards a sustainable, non-polluting, productive, profitable future where unemployment is minimal, if not non-existent, workers are happy, work is sufficiently rewarded and Class Level's are minimally apart.

Not only is the Peace And Prosperity of Humanity at stake, with potential colonization into the Universe, but the survival of Human Species.

Sustainable Development

To assist sustainable development, our patriarchal and imperialistic system of Government will have to fade. All major decisions will be made by voting in Free Democracy. Minor decisions will be made my elected representatives. Voting is mandatory for all Citizen's. The double- check counter balance system of cabinets in the Netherlands can be used to debate issues and decide on things which cannot be voted on. Voting has to progress to Internet.

We must realize our role in the world. We are each Global Citizen's, each part of Human Species, not some Race which hates one another. We cannot use and abuse our land and world anyway we please, like rampant out-of-control Resource stripping by Government's and Corporation's. We must become part of the workings of the world and not separate from it... lest we suffer horribly by our intricate interconnection with it. If we do not understand our Environment then we will lead it to destruction and us along with it in our own apocalypses. We are just a strand in the web of life and must behave wisely or the whole Timeline will go to the Hell's again.

Production, manufacturing and any other forms of development which imbalance the land and inhibit self-sustainment, which rape, plunder, pillage and murder the world will be prohibited. Such will require modification throughout the 21st Century.

Development of Science with Philosophy's and Religion's is crucial. Much of the youth have even become oblivious to morals stating such has no meaning in the 21st Century. The system will collapse upon itself if we cannot achieve strong foundations from a solid, diverse, usable knowledge and application of such of the world (and Universe) around us. We may, as some brag about, have Near-Enlightenment or Enlightenment with all the theoretical information on Internet but it most certainly is not applied correctly. In fact, many Nation's still don't even have Internet for the majority of their people or is badly censured!

All our Resources come from Nature. Until we get off Planet Earth and even get out of the Solar System, it is relatively very limited. Humanity is presently busy eating itself to obesity and drinking itself dry.

More materials can be made with a greater diverse knowledge of Science and Technology, like the invention of replaceable parts with metals and plastics. With this, Resources can be more efficiently harvested, maintained, altered, sold, all of which leads to higher profits. A large portion of the budget must go into Science, Technology, Information Technology, Philosophy and Religion. If levels of scientific and philosophical advancements are achieved where the vast majority of the populations of Planet Earth live in comfort, if not riches, then we will have succeeded.

Quite the opposite is happening in the beginning of the 21st Century. Everyone is keeling over dead left, right, middle and center. War's, revolutions and collapsing of Governments and Economy's is taking place. Major natural disasters are frequent. Many countries even have no democratic voting procedures.

I explore how to go about this in all my essays; where is a theoretical model by others which can be applied? We have none, it is ad hoc living thrown to the winds of failing international financial markets and all those swept along: All systems are based in previous centuries written by classicists and we can only modify, not rewrite.

Scientific and philosophical advancements should be given to the public; major decisions on their implementation should be given to vote. If people in the population fail to understand the new advancements, due to lack of proliferation of information, they will fall behind and hinder the rest. Not to mention, with an uninformed public who can make an intelligent vote? Thus we still have only the weak and corrupted representatives who presume and assume to know why they were elected.

There must be emphasis on better communication and technological advances, especially between different Cultures, Races and Species; we only dominate upon lower Species when we are very much connected on our dinner plate.

Without a Global Economy there is *no* Economy whatsoever.

To assist in the widespread, equitable and stable development of our Country into a sustainable, non-polluting, productive, profitable condition, a large emphasis on Education must exist. The public will be kept up-to-date and increasingly more knowledgeable so decision making and voting on important issues will be more intelligent and wise. The present conditions in High School's and the Hyvescool Rift between post-education is atrocious, all we here from our siblings is 'boring boring boring' and when can I go home and play my 3D Game and/or Film's on Internet with computers and smartphones. Even during class we hear in International New's that's all they do.

At present the Education System is going down in quality and increasing in price. Some studies leave you with $100,000 - $400,000 debt at the end! This will lead to a modern symptom ten times worse than the Feudal Ages with nobility rich and all the peasants starving. It will also decrease the availability of much needed higher skilled workers. Since there is no such thing as unskilled labor in 21st Century this will spiral downwards into even more unemployment; where are much needed retraining courses? Nowhere, the money only goes into rich private pockets again…

In addition to achieving our own goal, we must be able to associate with other Country's. To maintain the identity we have chosen we must be competitive. Economically speaking, this means we must maintain greater export revenues and internal revenues than import revenues; a company whose purchasing exceeds its earnings soon goes bankrupt… Our tools to be competitive are Credit, Resources, Territory (future sources of capital) and people (maintaining capital and identity). This does not mean stomp the neighbor, if they have olives and we have oil then conduct Trade and not War. War does not help Trade as much as you think, look at the U.S. Deficit now due to such far out in left field War's for oil. Look now at Palestine and Israel in rubble who could have been trading the whole time. How much does that cost?

We have to work towards Free Democracy and Free Economy, which does not mean everything for 'free' on Internet and if you download only two demos you get 175 spyware on your computer. That is just outrageous. How am I supposed to know if I can use the program and want to buy it if I don't get to try a limited free version??!

Credit, as stated here in a previous essay, does not mean massive debts which will *never* be recovered from. That's why they then go to War with false hopes they'll find gold and it spirals down even further into only a feverish Gold Rush Effect. It does not mean the impoverishing of the people in enslavement which won't be recovered from for even a century. It does not mean the playing around with fake non-existing virtual money investments. It does not mean the raping of our one single Planet…

At our present rate of self-destruction will also just all be dead before we even get off Planet in some nightmare post-apocalypse scenario where a few walled cities only survive with a few Elite Scientist's.

Or, how about put a large wall around Europe, England and Canada… The rest will all just die and deprecate.

With the present greed and corruption of our Government's, Corporation's, Royal Family's and Elite Individual's in the beginning of the 21st Century, not to mention the total waste on useless War's, such a scenario is becoming even very likely.

What will happen when the oil runs out and there are no electrical installments?

What will happen when pollution goes unchecked?

What will happen with uncontrolled epidemics?

We are now in 2014, even back then, seeing it every day in International New's.

Farm and Fishing

If fishing is being overproduced, in England there was even a loss of 100000 fishing jobs in recent history, it should be put to vote on how to reduce it and by how much. Recommended is to create many clean and controlled fish farms instead of devouring the lakes and seas until they are empty.

Interestingly, enough the exact opposite is the case with farming. We have, due to things like genetic modification, a huge surplus of food. The reality of the Politics has to figure out the moral, ethical and economical reasons why we are not helping other poorer countries with such. At present, it gets thrown into Black Hole Effect disaster regions and though humanitarian it does not help the longer term goal of also rebuilding such countries into sustainable development.

Also vast amount of food which are on date in supermarkets and restaurants are thrown out every day. ·

To keep prices artificially inflated the same is done.

Energy

To assist in our goal of sustainable, productive, non-polluting, profitable living, renewable, competitive, non-polluting and profitable sources of Energy must be developed. There is only an increase in the demand.

There is also no reason why the Arab Tycoon's cannot simply invest in such, take ownership and make even more money in the future as Humanity colonizes the Solar System by using *all* forms of alternative Energy.

Clean energy, or better known as Green Energy, does work. It, in fact, is even far more modern and advanced. The ISS uses solar panels and Germany has major investments in Solar Energy. With other hyper modern possibilities like even residual Energy, EM Fields and just good old gravity the actual quantity and quality of energy in the Universe is either Near-Infinite or Infinite.

This, of course, does not mean it's free. You still need all the people and devices to deliver such.

Energy does work. On an individual scale, sufficient joules of Energy must be usable by the body. Recommended to each individual is to increase their bodily efficiency of energy absorption so that their productive output can be maximized. Carbohydrates and sugars provide a good source of energy and regular exercise with proteins provides the proper base and structure for optimal usage of such Energy.

Renewable meat, dairy products, grains, vegetables, legumes, beans, fruits, nuts and seeds is probably a good diverse ratio. This will also assist in the longevity of a Citizen's productive years. What do we eat on average in the north: 1 brown piece of meat, soggy potatoes, and dead cooked vegetables, that to go along with high cholesterol, fat, salt and protein breakfasts, lunches and snacks. It's no wonder.

Drugs And Alcohol

The abuse of social drugs and alcohol should be controlled.

The excessive prescribing of pharmaceuticals in trial and error band aid treatments, which never target the cause nor cure the patient, need to be modernized.

All of such things have to do with the Energy in your system. You are effectively hanging yourselves with your own system, defining one thing with the left hand and stabbing with the right hand…

On a societal level it works much the same way: As above so below.

The microcosmic reflects the macrocosmic.

All bodies in the Universe are governed by the same laws.

Research And Development

We must research and develop a lot more, through large investment, the sources of Power and Energy which Nature, and GOD, has given to Humanity. Sun, EM Field's, Solar, Wind, Water and plain gravity are inherent in the Universe and highly available. Only backward outdated Politic's and Economy's prevent such from developing.

Other sources of Geo-Thermal Energy can be the heat within Planet Earth.

There is also Fusion and Fission, the latter now completely ignored, with the resulting deadly radiation and is being misused by Russia as we speak. They're even in high demand with computer and Internet connected systems selling another 100 new models. In America there are also over a hundred in operation. It's more like we're on the verge of a global meltdown scenario.

It is recommended to focus a hell of a lot more on non-polluting, infinitely available, easy to locate and relatively inexpensive sources of Energy.

Fossil fuels should die with the 20th Century but statistics state otherwise: Everyone because of your car is still highly dependent, 3 billion still use wood and charcoal to cook and generate heat. With dwindling forests and rain forests the size of Greece per year consumed and 2 million barrels per day pumped out of Canada you have got to ask yourself if they've all lost their bananas.

If Nature has given us these obvious forms, why search elsewhere? It is foolish and economically unsound to invest in hard-to-reach, hard-to-use, non-renewable and environmentally destructive sources of energy.

We have all the Element's in the Universe to use now, there is no excuse left.

Modern Industrialization And Foreign Investment

All present industry which does not support our projected goal throughout the 21st Century will be gradually replaced. This needs to be assisted and subsidized in a correct fashion, not another 100 billion blown on wasted IT projects of which 1 in 10 succeeded, if any.

Foreigners are exactly that: Strangers, people of a different kin who are trying to make their country work. Some will not be interested in how we go about things. Our goal is to gain strength, identity, autonomy, independence, self-sustainment towards a sustainable, non-polluting, productive, profitable future, not power and enslavement.

Each case of foreigners should be judged separately on an interview-presentation basis. It is very important we keep a strong hold on our Country and maintain our projected identity, otherwise the Chinese will also own 51% of all our real estate, not just Canada. It is, therefore, recommended no more than 40% of anything in our country can be owned by foreign investors. At present it's a Split Up Pie Effect and we have no say over anything. Each other Country does whatever they want to without any effective governing body. The recent fiasco leading to War in Ukraine is a perfect example where they just put sanctions on each other and everyone loses.

Now there is another split East and West block which is in violation of Marco Polo and we pay even €543 per kilo for some spices. That's absurd.

The prime bases of our Economy, such as resources, will also be restricted in such a way. Education, Research and Development, Science, Technology, Philosophy and Religion has also become global, especially with Internet, but it is very foolish just to give such things away to a foreign Country. If you think ripping on Internet is bad these days, think of industrial espionage. The loss of potential profit is probably even more than the Entertainment Industry. If there is an excess or outdate in such key sectors of the country then we will gladly share them, for a price... Such a price does not per se, within Free Democracy, have to be only a dollar or euro value. I'll give you data and you give me spices: All trade to date was based on this fact.

Polaris in Polaris, our icy citadel fortress in the north of Canada with Near-Infinite Defense System's, though far from the ideal of the fully isolated utopian Elite Spaceship, will make a strong effort to invest in such key sectors and in things we do not yet possess and things which are world common, world renowned and which represent a world trend, as long as they are not in contradiction to the primary goals.

We will trade with many Country's as Global Citizen's in all sectors with the purpose of increasing our diversity and openness, which also do not contradict the primary goals. This will enrich all our sectors greatly and the benefits to our economy can be manifold.

Our goals are not only necessary to evolve Humanity but to progress in Peace And Prosperity, not just survive, half-starving, on piecemeal. Polaris has no problem with other countries as long as we can maintain our own identity and goal, equal rights in world ventures and rights to grant our Citizen's the bias in economic negotiations which exist on our realm of influence i.e. our territory. By granting us these rights, we equally grant other countries the same if they will. If they do not than there is not much point in relations.

Our motto could be: Equal in Return.

In terms of Immigration, a highly debated issue in the beginning of the 21st Century, we will most certainly not adopt WWII neo-nazi racist and discriminatory measures such as blind deportation. The total illogic of such after the Country let them in in the first instance could be recorded in the History of Humanity as one the biggest blunders ever made next to the end of colonization.

We are going to colonize Mars, right? Right, yah, eh, totally!

We, however, will not allow the other extreme of another Mongol Invasion of Europe. It's like Ghengis Khan never actually failed… There most sit leeching off of the State.

We cannot also gladly allow all refugees, those brought to unlivable conditions by the inadequacy of their Government's, to enter our country in unlimited numbers according to quantity and quality of available jobs and only if they have some way of sustaining themselves or are capable of being educated. There is, after all, in the 21st Century no such thing as unskilled labor in Polaris, either. This will then be allowed only for a period of time. After such a period of time they must begin contributing as a skilled worker to the development of our Country. We will not burden our system with poorly organized welfare, leading to communist states, and homeless and criminals on the street. The length of time should be voted on. If they cannot contribute, in any way, then they will be deported back from whence they came, or if that is impossible, to a less developed neighbouring Country where they may be productive. Why don't they send them to an equally unskilled or less skilled labor Country where they can find jobs?

The burden of the world is not solely ours.

We must save those who have already come here.

Criminals should be reintegrated, not given a death sentence.

Homeless should be given cheap housing.

With 4 million+ of such in America alone, it is no surprise what the resulting Chaos is.

A Citizen in Polaris is one who is born in Polaris, is being educated and/or reintegrated to work in Polaris, a paid or volunteer worker in Polaris who is assisting development of and maintaining of our goal.

People who have worked in Polaris for a minimal period of time will be given additional financial assistance and/or education if they happen to be out of work.

How few Country's follow even these Basic Guidelines?? What happened to Order? In the past you would live with your family on a farm, now it's get kicked out or get the hell out asap.

Immigrants of more stable countries will be rarely accepted; why come here?

Visitor's, Government and Corporate Official's, CEO's, Tourist's, Celebrity's are welcome for longer periods of time since they already have the Credit to do so. The blatant banning of such Investor's due to sanctions is also a bad trend these days.

The point of Immigration is to promote our goals.

Tax

In a system of total Capitalism, tax does not even exist. This, of course, is just another unreachable extreme. With all things mentioned it can be seen there is the continued attempt to raise the standard of living to one where such things as Sickness And Disease, Unemployment, Crime, Black Money and other downfalls of each system are eliminated.

Such a Utopia is also probably only ever possible on that fully isolated Elite Colony Space Ship. But then, 100 Light Years out, Alien's suddenly come along on a routine patrol and blow it to kingdom come. Due to the inability to read the warning signal being broadcasted they did not know they were entering enemy territory…

Besides those expenditures, however, are the Public Works, the common utilities which all citizens use such as Sewage, Parks, Garbage, System Maintenance, rolling sidewalks, robots, cyborgs, defense laser turrets and last but not least the Laser Military… Should the Laser Military not also be turning a profit? Is this a Smart or Stupid Question?

It is technically possible to have each citizen take care of their own lot and prevent the degradation of the national debt and Public Works. However, until each citizen gains a higher standard of living in the never reachable American Dream, having Tax for these purposes is superior.

Any way you look at it, though, Tax is too easily used and abused by so-called Social Government's. The sheer ludicrousness of placing 70% tax rates on richer Citizen's just drives them all away to a house in France: In NL we pay about that amount.

Therefore, Polaris will implement high abstract mathematics by Elite Scientist's and Economist's to find the right balance. How many are listened to these days except at International New's stations? How many are implemented?

So many systems do not have enough balance.

You have to be careful, in your own opposition, you do not enter a greater extreme.

Modes

A couple more theoretical modular propositions:

The necessary Credit's for all Free Services will be paid by each citizen for what they use. This will be paid by the citizen just as though shopping for food; the Citizen will know how much they are paying for the apples and how much for the oranges. There will be no hidden taxes.

Each citizen will know exactly the payments of the Country, where the Credit's are going to and for what. Done in categories, there is no comprising of sensitive data since such should not be sensitive data, thus where is our transparency of bureaucracy?

There will be maintenance of the Government to prevent surrendering too much power to the population, to each Citizen, the nature of a self-governing Country. A Government not in control is only Anarchy, however a Government which does not grant their people power is also not a Democracy.

This is not Capitalism, Socialism, Communism, Fascism, Dictatorship or Despotism, it is a type of Democracy called Free Democracy. Most likely, Humanity will struggle throughout the 21st Century with various types of Democracy holding fake neck-to-neck elections, granting false hope to suffering populations and lead to more deficits bound by the whim of the all-powerful 7 Block or 14 Block on Planet Earth as it too is split in too many multiple factions causing only more deluge and despair and death.

After all, if your government like America even did at the beginning of the 20th Century, does not turn a profit, more income then expenditure, then there is evidently something wrong with the system.

The system itself, therefore, will not be static and can change.

This is Polaris

With the successful implementation of the recommended guidelines throughout the 21st Century, Polaris should turn into a sustainable, non-polluting, productive, profitable and thereby, a peaceful and happy place to live. The vast majority would be satisfied and the environment would not collapse around us.

The only way this cannot work is if Corporation's, Government's, Royal Family's, Elite Individual's and Peoples refuse to communicate and cooperate with each other towards such a sustainable, non-polluting, productive, profitable future. Yet, that is the only thing we see in International New's: Conflict, disagreement, strife, prejudice and racism.

Not only is the Peace And Prosperity of Humanity at stake with colonization into the Universe but the survival of Human Species...

Responsibility

As long as each citizen performs a Society Function then they can live in that Society. Such a position comes with a certain measure of responsibility. This, however, due to Seakness And Disease and handicaps is not particularily realizable; also age plays an important factor in the Society Production.

With the advance of all Types Of Technology, job functions will not decrease, money will not be harder to get, and there will be, as is now, a shifting of the Type Of Job's. Instead of the machine taking over your job, you will be involved with the machine in some way. So, where some jobs disappear, others will appear. This, however, due to the impracticality of retraining workers in an ever more complicated future Society has led to more unemployment in beginning of 21st Century...

Do you really want to go back to no washing machines, no fridges and no other multi-functional devices on some pristine idealistic farm? See Walddorf.

Science and Technology is meant to take away the tedious, monotonous, unpleasurable and/ or dangerous jobs. By that reasoning and fact, jobs will remain which are not displeasurable to humans. Thereby, the jobs which will be available will be suitable to human involvement. However, once again, due to increase in idleness and highly trained functions which have become the vast majority of functions only the younger generation will benefit from these advances which we worked for: They have better certificates, diplomas, educations and are a hell of a lot cheaper! They also have god-like stamina to get up and do do a 12+ hour day every day in hybrid autos like I remember in my good ole MCSE'er days doing even outsourcing.

Another one of the critical errors made back in primarily the 70's with Immigration was the concept of unskilled Labor. In the 21st Century in Modern Western Civilization there is no such thing as unskilled Labor.

Now, you might like the job you have, but you are forced to survive. Or, just jump off a Tokyo balcony... The joke is here, of course, that they have no balconies due to too much wind factors...

With improved Education there will be more and more attractive likable opportunities for people. At present you have an increase in the cost and a decrease in the quality of Education. Another major problem, which I might discuss in another essay, is the massive rift between high school and post degrees though I have mentioned in multiple times in other works too. With the loan you need to pay for one, you are also near-instantly enslaved by Society. It is, actually, completely illogical to not extend the Education of your own People so they can get a paid job...

I've been doing unpaid jobs and projects every day in NL since 2003 CE, allowing for Sickness and Disease.

Each of us must contribute to something in Society. It does not matter what for we each have a Relative IQ in each Relative Sector. See previous essays here.

This is the beauty of Credit or Money, it is a completely objective Tool, satisfying its own system. Unfortunately, it is in subjective hands. And, obviously, one can never go back to a primarily barter Black Market System. Think alone of all the Black Money with no tax on it...

It is possible for everyone, definitely with Internet these days, to become a millionaire. Back in previous centuries there was an even farther rift between classes and the total lack of opportunity for the vast majority of all people. Very often, all your sons would just be drafted into the next war for GOD, King and Country.

So, theoretically and potentially, you can be a complete frozen flavored popsicle bum and still get rich at some point.

If you perform some Society Function and do not break the Law then you can do what you want. Though such may be limited, think even of the entire Planet Earth as microscopic and nanoscopic in the entire Universe and you are just one dot...

'Know your lines from your limitations.'

'Know the f'in line from the f'in limit.'

'How else could a system work? Someone has to clean the dishes...'

The trouble with Modern Society these days is it does not know the balance needed in each and every system anymore; the very Ecosystem needs balance to survive and we are an intricate interconnected part of such.

Humanity has overstepped its bounds and is ripping, leeching and killing the Planet for short term profit goals with no sustainable development. In addition to such, Modern Western Civilization, with the exception of Internet, is not particularly willing, generous and/or open to share and/or help others with similar development, Science and Technology. We donate more eagerly to War's to ensure Oil, their peoples have still not been saved and now the East is starting to leech the West as prime real estate investment and reverse colonization buying up our ownerships with International Stock's, Multinational Corporation's, Government Loan's, Bank Deal's and we just keep conducting more War's upon them. Why do we have to be the World Watch Dog and not earn from it? Despite such arguments of them coming from a post WWII Scenario we are 'ownly' making large financial losses and State Debt's aren't dropping either. We need to kill the War Machine and not the potential consumer, especially not existing ones with highly exaggerated sanctions like a bunch of Teenager's fighting it out.

'There they went and blew up another Open Market to get at shadowy terrorists.'

'Talking about missing the Tourist Potential...'

One of the greatest atrocities heard to date was the cost of Medicine for other Country's, they were literally told to buy our shit... you, yourself, also get given stupendous health bills, another 125000 get fired in personnel rather than middles and methods again and the Government pays for their Welfares.

These things all contribute towards a Downward Spiral Effect.

Economy must be the primary driving motivation in the 21ˢᵗ Century, not War which primarily divides, destroys and demolishes, it only unites for a short time.

Even better than asking 'what is War good for' is to ask what all of those Wars resulted in. Technically, Germany has all of its Territory back and is one of the strongest Economy's in the world, now. That was done by ending such repetitive War's. After WWII, they apparently even worked 6 days per week, the pendulum has swung back to a somewhat Left Labor Party, but then we find out in International New's again that most of their Truck Chauffeur Salary's are only €400 per month as they hire Eastern Europe Block Member's.

And talking about missing the Trade potential… who even wants to visit those regions where some rocket may just blast over… or straight into your Appartment's. To date War has been fought with rampaging Army's but seriously why do you have to aim at civilian buildings? Weapon's in *all* their homes, not just mosques? That's a bad joke.

All their Women and Children and Elder's made homeless is no ones solution. It's always about Money and they are your future work force, a present work force now desecrated like some mad God's swinging at each other wildly for domination in a really great 3D Game. Hollywood Film's portray this well too.

In the 21ˢᵗ Century, primarily due to modernization, there are an out-of-control exponentially increasing and accelerating quantity and quality of Society Problem's. Everyone has, in some way, contributed to such in one degree or another and there is never and always no Money to solve such problems.

Who cleans up Planet Earth? Who pollutes Planet Earth?

Do not blame only your Corporation's and Government's. They did not make you buy 2.6 cars per household and counting… They did not use your Credit Card for the whole house under plastic and now you have to pay 3 years later… That was even decades ago, a type of corporate marketing under the false pretenses of Liberalization led to more and more enslavement. So by such Logic, the Arab's have to solve it for us…

Pointing fingers and giving blame is futile. Without the effort towards the solution, it will also never happen.

Who pays for the damages done? Who pays for the repairs?

Each of us have littered and polluted. Who picks up the garbage?

Each of us have eaten meat and killed in some way. Who regrows the cattle?

Ask yourself, with all your Material Acquisition's, how many things or creatures had to actually be destroyed or killed for such.

Think of Trees alone…

'It is so hard to create, so easy to destroy…'

In Free Democracy, if it is a Society Problem which Pollution is then the entire Society must contribute. One is only responsible for what one causes. Yet, every time Tax is brought up at Election's there is a resounding 'Boooooo…' Well, if I told you that I have lived off of only an average of €10000 per year for my entire time in Netherlands since 1996 then would you believe me? We need to invest in our own Economy and like it or not we're not in Cybertronic Age yet so such runs off of People. Unfortunately, now we're each just an expendable Resource.

There is no such thing as Non-Violence in the entire Universe. At some point, the Ganymede Galaxy, Andromeda Galaxy and the Milky Way will actually all collide with each other. If one has any conception of Hell then that is truly Inferno.

To put water in the wine, something I practice more often recently, there is a difference between senseless violence and violence with a purpose. Violence is more of a force of change which can be used for Good, Neutral and/or Evil. It's also more like just various shades of gray...

What is your own personal violence...

'He who throws the first stone is usually the husband of the Jewish wife.'

Not all 'chinks', 'japs' and 'muslim mongols' are the Enemy.

If we do not conduct cooperation, Trade and Economy, on a global scale with all Country's instead of practicing Warfare and various illegal competitions then the future will not be so pretty for anyone. They keep forgetting the internal rising of the People.

The purpose of Competition was to reduce price and increase quality. In practice, in the 21st Century, especially in Information Technology it has proven just to wipe out the vast majority who make any Money or Credit, relatively no more than 1/10 of endeavors actually make it temporarily in projects with no more fixed lasting incomes and fast personnel shifting. Picture it as the worst Type Of Liberal Corporation Scenario.

Likewise, out of the whole percentage of Artist's and Author's only a tiny percentage even makes one single red cent.

How is Tax actually being spent?

It is being used to subsidize meat. The meat you buy is much more expensive than you think and you are paying more than you think. This increases the cost of the system.

'The taste of freedom...'

The vast majority in Modern Western Civilization actually goes to Youth, Handicap's, Sickness And Disease, Elderly which is already 75% of the entire population. I don't need to even argue anything else...

It is being wasted on International Warfare of which no results and/or profit come from. It then increases the National Debt and the cost on the Modern Western Civilization to zillions even while we turn into iso-clones in iso-pods.

Your tax, which they do not even tell you, is being spent on a large quantity and quality of projects which also result in no profit and/or results.

Meanwhile, we get to sit in most Country's on poor Welfare, bad Hellth System's and little or no prospect of paid work. With credit cards, eating your savings, watching investments implode and inflation there is little 'cents' left.

Science and Technology can solve Society Problem's with Mercury, Tetrachlorothylene, Hexachlorobenzyne, Sulfur Dioxide and Nitrogen Dioxide but Politic's, Money and Credit do not allow so.

Bio-Chemical's should not be underestimated these days. You, too, can be volatilized, absorbed, deposited as wet or dry deposition, parted, transferred, diffused and suspended. Nothing like Osmosis!

Literally, after the trees when the phytoplankton go straight southwards you might as well close the last chapter on Humanity.

Not much exists to prevent your exposure. Through the use of Oxidant's which tend to create chemical by-products, dirty water can be coagulated, flocculated and put through sedimentation so as to be finally filtered. The result, however, is a sludge of slimy, stinking, fuming, toxic waste which can be disposed of somewhere... Water is primarily chosen and in a lot of places bottle water costs more than the enslavement benzene.

Therefore, we have the term 'Re-moval' of waste written into even Law's. It does not delete the waste, it merely transfers it some other location in a somewhat different form, still toxic and poisonous. The half-life of Bio-Chemical's like chlorinated compounds, base compounds, acid compounds and radiated compounds is just mind boggling. Various materials also last even centuries.

'Now we want to throw Nukes at each other again...'

'Well, weeeeee, good luck finding more places to dump all your garbage!'

'Or, geeeeee, why don't we just burn up the whole atmosphere at the same time!'

Better solutions are not impossible and these are definitely not through War which draws a lot of Money away from other Sector's in the Economy. The best to date is probably the naturally occurring bacteria which eat garbage, mostly plastic. Only very recently, in 2009 did Netherlands offer public bins to recycle plastic. And also a smart Student came up with the idea to pump it out and recycle it into much needed plastic which the demand of has sky-rocketed.

If Science and Technology does not solve its own advanced problem then no one else will.

Science and Technology can also theoretically dissolve and eliminate Bio-Chemical's with other ones. Good luck however succeeding at that with the cigarettes in your lungs, the benzene in your cells, the fat layers all covering it up and presto more SAD and MAD and DAD can you please pay for my Student Loan...

The cause of something is very seldom looked at, thus no cures.

Companies have to stop producing them. People have to stop putting money into them.

Reduction and Elimination are the all-important countermeasures here.

The chance of effective antidotes is almost nihil. When poisoned, can you get to the antidote, do they have the right antidote and how long does it take to heal?

Now they even want to experiment on Human's with Genetic Modification. Woohoo! Mutant War's here we come again!

The air which we breathe is being polluted. The earth which we feed from is being polluted. The sun which stimulates all things is now killing us with excessive UV. The water which we drink is being poisoned.

Greed and corruption through Money and Credit and War prevents such solutions in 99.9%+ of all cases.

'If we pay this much then why are we not being cured?'

Some Society Problem's are, of course, not easy to solve. However, if we do not take serious measures now in the beginning of the 21st Century then we will all have a far greater problem on our hands.

'Ignoring the problem never solves it.'

'Just like Cancer, if you wait too long, it can never be cured again.'

Responsibility, therefore, is the duty of each and every citizen from the Grocer to the CEO to the President.

'So much for the Will of Humanity…'

We must perceive ourselves as one Humanity on one Planet.

Even until 2056 CE or later there will be no one else… no one will hear our last dying whimper and in the vast Universe it might even be completely insignificant, except for one factor: Our role in the Universe in the future.

Once we colonize the stars then we will play a significant role through growth.

And our hierarchal Master's are not willing to pay for our Slaves…

This also means to pay for your own workers and invest in your own.

Objectivity VS Subjectivity

Objectivity vs Subjectivity in Russel's Problems of Philosophy is represented on several levels. Russell's overall attempt is to bring this into perspective with Objectivity holding the upper hand. For how else can we see the Objective Truth?

By Objectivity we are referring to an Omniscient point of view. By Subjectivity we indicate the limited mind set.

Russel defines these terms by, respectively, Description vs Acquaintance, Physical Object vs Sense Data, Public Space vs Private Space, General or Universal vs Particular, Deduction vs Induction, and A Priori vs A Posteriori. In a broader perspective it is Rationalism vs Empiricism.

In the world of Rationalist's, the world is 'permanent, unchanging, timeless'. Though it is well understood the limited mind cannot perceive this perfection, the very definition alone show it's Objectivity. With Plato's support Russell shows that Space, a primarily Rationalist conception, is for real; whether the distance between two Object's is measured or not does not qualify their existence, they still exist.

Empiricism, rather, denies such 'Idealistic' tendencies and enjoys the ceaseless change occurring in the particular. They hold such Objective realms do not exist and rather we can only rely on Descartes, 'Cogito Ergo Sum'. Rationalist's would respond, 'Sum Merito Cogito'.

In the beautiful realm of Quality's and Relation's, not just Quantity's and Number's, A Priori knowledge is free from limited minds coming in and tainting them. They persist in whatever splendid colors they surely have for they are determined by the nature of things and not one person's will. We have all of these, Emotion's, Feeling's, and Love, and there is no machine which can measure such.

A Posteriori is quite different. This states one can only know anything after experiencing it, thus I could quantify your Experience. So, in effect we must go through a trial and error process in our entirely Subjective Reality's, ever capable of using a Method System for any such thing resulting would immediately become outdated. We then are forced to come to our own Subjective conclusions. This is the belief in a world ruled by Chaos by excessive Materialism rather than Order with A Priori in too much Idealism.

In Deductive Knowledge a system is shown to exist. There is such a thing as 2 + 2 = 4. We call it such, however those differences exist. Is two separate chairs one or two? We can clearly show they are separate. With Deduction we can take such quantitative generalities and apply them to other generalities such as other furniture or other particulars, such as other separate chairs. By grouping things into larger Category's of a common trait things are generally simplified and we can then work from these general Category's to simplify our lives.

Induction, meanwhile, asks you to access all those million points and then tell us. This, as Russell, shows, has an inherent problem: by relying solely on Experience you can never absolutely prove anything and even gaining probability of something recurring demands many recurrences. Though things work this way, there is no reason to be forced to understand them in such a way. One cannot access the Omniscient and Omnipoten, Objective Point Of View and deduct from there.

'If we could only hold this vision for a moment...'

'A glimpse of the Eye Of God is everything...'

'One moment in Eternity and we see it all...'

'Praise GOD.'

'Hail Allah.'

This discussion naturally flows along to General or Universal Reality's. Generalities can be drawn from General to General, or from General to Particular, or from Particular to Particular, thus so many particularities. This has its advantages as shown in Deduction.

Particular's, as in Induction, go from Particular to Particular, or from Particular to General. Thus, they lack Objectivity, existing in the Subjective they are bound to error.

Public Space has many suppositions to it. Liebniz suspects the monad; all things. To the minutest are possessed of Consciousness. Berkely sees the mind of GOD. Hagel holds there is a Collective Consciousness of all things. Russell prefers to see it in terms of Science, or as we are discussing, Rationalism. There is a definite Geometry to Object's in Space. This is where they exist. The combination of all these Object's determines the whole, or Public Space. This order applies equally to Time and Space. This is obviously Pure Reality which is superior to our limited Private Spaces.

Virtual Private Space gives us a correspondence to the Real Public Space. We are in the inferior realm of separate points of view. We are possessed with an angle here, a shadow there, an intimation here, however the Physical Object in itself remains illusive.

The Physical Object, that great Perfect Pbject in Object-ivity, does exist, according to Russell. We can only know in our present state of development the correspondence with it, the Sense Data. Russell holds its reality by refuting the Idealist's in one statement: The act of perceiving is separate from the Object being perceived.

This is not impossible since the Object is simply what it is and what we make of it is often Nonsense Ad Absurdum.

'Do you see the same table which I do?'

'Did we have a common experience?'

'Do you have the same perspective?'

Sense Data is the epitomical level of Subjectivity. The famous example of The Table cannot be refuted or denied; to each person, each from a different point of view, the table is not only a different touch, taste, smell, appearance, and sound, it is also a different shape! How can we possibly know the real thing? This demonstrates how shallow our assumptions of Reality really are.

To provide a possible solution, Russel provides the reality of Description. This is what we can use to simulate a measure of Omniscience, without which we are in dark tunnels. Not all things are necessary to be achieved through Empiricism, such is our own experience. We can learn of other things second hand from others. Though this demands their acquaintance with such things we can rely on it as a general source of knowledge, friendship, acquaintance and so forth.

Acquaintance is our experiencing of Sense Data. There are several levels which are worth mentioning, though inappropriate to go into detail in this essay. We are acquainted to things through Introspection (Inner World's), Memory of Sense Data (our Subjective and Objective Self). Between Objective and Subjective Reality we have glimpse into each one, now and zen, which we remember or we do not and we try to find each of our paths to Freedom, Peace and Illumination.

In conclusion, we can then ponder, what is Truth? Russell, after all of the above, goes into this. And, an even better question, how can we possibly know Truth? Though Russell is extraneously caught up in interwoven definitions he proffers a glimmer of hope with Acquaintance and Description, showing we may eventually achieve the Universal Comprehension! Let us each work towards this…

What is clearly demonstrated to us is the superiority of Objective Reality vs Subjective Reality, for our lives and existence which are regularly imperiled by Strife, War and Death upon us…

The Presocratic Philosopher's

Part 01

Philosophy begins with the Greek's because they were the first to use rational thought (in the West) to explain Nature; they used natural terminology to describe Nature. In this sense they also founded the beginnings of Science. The very word 'Phil-o-sophy', 'lover-of-wisdom' was invented by Pythagoras. Before the Greeks there was Mythology and Judaism, a purely divine way of looking at Nature. From this we see the originally Greek attempt to reconcile the lives of Mortal's with those of Immortal's. Rather than from the divine perspective Philosophy introduced Knowledge from the Human perspective. This short account will go into the evidence to support these claims.

Consistent with all the Pre-Socratic's is the usage of logic and evidence; this constitutes rational thought, as opposed to intuitive, magical means. The Milesian's discussed the Element's in various degrees showing how they were interrelated. This is most pronounced in Anaximander's famous fragment describing the coming and going of things from the eternal Apeiron. Heraclitus, a Nietschian fellow, rationalizes in fragment 23, 'It is in changing that things find repose.' The Eleatic's, with Zeno's dialectics, argue against change itself, showing it to be mere illusion. Though they may be highly abstract their arguments use logic and evidence. In response, Qualitative Pluralism fights for a balance between change and statical forms. Empedocles' fragment 20: 'These two forces, Strife and Love, existed in the past and will exist in the future; nor will boundless Time, I believe, ever be empty of the pair.' Atomism reduces the argument to the interaction of void and particles of matter. Pythagoras applies Rationality to a way of life. Even the Sophist's who disagree with absolute realities must use the method of logic and evidence to debate, and they do it very well. So, in the creation of Philosophy (in the West), the combining of observed phenomena into systematic interpretations of Nature, we also see the beginning of a Universal Methodology i.e. Science.

The most obvious demonstration of why the Greeks begun Philosophy is because one of them, Pythagoras, invented the word. This tends to indicate origins. The word itself is an extension, or maybe even the basis, of the previous paragraph. To love Wisdom is to be on the search for Truth. Thus, the source is in the very definition, something the Greeks greatly appreciated.

Before all of this rationalization occurred, people were somewhat content to worship rather than analyze. Possibly, it was more digestible to do so. Xenophanes, one of the earliest Pre-Socratic's was the first to blast this away with his Rational Theology i.e. fragments 1-10: 'Homer and Hesiod attributed to the gods all sorts of actions which when done by men are disreputable and deserving of blame -such lawless deeds as theft, adultery, and mutual deception.' Here he renounces Homer and Hesiod. To explain the 'true nature' of God's, Goddesses and GOD, he puts them into the Human context: 'If oxen's or lions had hands which enable them to draw and paint pictures as men do, they would portray their gods having bodies like their own; horses would portray them as horses, oxen as oxen.' Appropriately enough, as is the case with some other Pre-Socratic's, he was banished from his native city of Colophon.

From this, we see a continuing trend in later Pre-Socratic's to describe Nature from the human perspective. In effect, they attempt to reconcile the Divine with the Human. In this is the largest downfall of Mythology and Judaism which made no such attempts; their mandate was 'Obey or Die'. Attempting an analysis of the divine compared to us is infinitely more useful. A couple examples of this are T5 of Leucippus, 'In the All, which is infinite, the full and the void are what we call the elements...' and, fragment 40 of Heraclitus, 'The fairest universe is but a heap of rubbish piled up at random.' Crude maybe but Modern Quantum Chaos Theory supports it. A primarily philosophical function, the Pre-Socratic's attempted to reconcile divine and mortal similarities and differences. As in fragment 12 of Empedocles, 'Hear first the four roots of all things: shining Zeus, life giving Hera, Aidoneus, and Nestis who with her tears fills the springs from which mortals draw their life.'

In total, we can see the Greeks truly did introduce novelty on several levels. These novelties are Philosophy.

Part 02

To quote Wheelwright, '(The Eleatic School) represents the first all-out-attempt in the Western World to establish pure reason, with its demands of logical consistency and relatedness, as the sole criterion of truth.' So Parmenides is a turning point in Pre-Socratic Philosophy. Before, Philosophy was being determined by the mere opinions of various enlightened shamanic individuals.

Parmenides was not interested in the mere Observation's of a select few: Fragment 9, '...For men have established the habit of naming two thought forms; therein they have erred, because one of the thought forms ought not to be named...' The random criterion for a system such as Anaximander's Apeiron and Element's, was insufficient. According to Parmenides there has to be strict categories; if one cannot apply everything into two sub-sections, it simply is not. As in fragment 7A, '...Necessarily therefore, it simply Is or it simply Is Not.' Apparently, hand-in-hand with this are the notions: 1. Being is One 2. Being is Unchanging. The correlation between Is, and being is One is unclear, being developed only later by Melissus in fragments 5-10 i.e. fragment 8, 'If there existed a many, the many existing things would have to be of the same kind as the One is...' Parmenides vaguely eludes to this supposition in fragment 7E, 'Since there has to be limit, Being is complete on every side, like the mass of a well-rounded Sphere, equally balanced in every direction from the center.' It is only in later testimonies where we get the interpretation of Is being equated to One. This is important, because how can one discuss Parmenides as a turning point if the interpretations do not correspond with his fragments?

Possibly all is not lost, and we can still demonstrate the turning point by showing Parmenides' demand for an absolute system which is logically self-sustaining. This can be done if we see that his two categories, Is and Is Not, provide a basis for irrefutable Logic. The way to go about this is simple. One cannot deny that everything exists. To do otherwise is to deny Existence. Since the act of denying demands your existence, you have just contradicted yourself. That was an example of reductio ad absurdum, or dialectical syllogism, the way Zeno argued. In this way we can see a different manifestation of the strict logical categorization as expressed by Zeno. In such a method Zeno adheres to the Is and Is Not axiom. Melissus, on the other hand, took Is and Is Not and turned it into Is and What It Seems To Be. As in fragment 8, '…Now in our everyday life we assume that we see and hear and understand more or less rightly…' In all, it is impossible to take Parmenides alone in the question of him being a turning point. A comprehensive account of his fellows, as just given, is also necessary.

In the axioms 1. Being is One and 2. Being is Unchanging, presuming interpretations are accurate, we can see his strict adherence to two fundamentals. Thus, pure reason is being demanded. However, to counteract the 'experts' again, how can we call an arbitrary designation of two categories by Parmenides as 'logical consistency and relatedness'? If the axioms are wrong, so is all the rest.

In summation, if Wheelwright is correct, and if mere adherence to your presumptions (axioms) constitutes 'pure reason as the sole criterion of truth', then, and only then, Parmenides can be considered a turning point in Pre-Socratic Philosophy.

Part 03

The replies to Parmenides come from 5 sources: Qualitative Pluralism, Atomism, Pythagoreanism, Plato and Aristotle. The differences will be shown between the first three and agreement will rest with the Pythagorean's.

Parmenides holds 1. Being Is 2. Being is Unchanging and/or 1. Being is One 2. One is Many (see previous Question). Empedocles and Anaxagoras consider a monistic view as inaccurate. To them the axioms 1. Qualities are Plural 2. Qualities are eternal 3. Qualities are intermixed. Leucippus and Democritus reduce it to two: 1. Qualities are obscure knowledge 2. Atoms and void are real knowledge. Pythagoras brings it to one: 1. All things come from the number One, including the opposites.

The view of Pythagoras encompasses greater quantities of variables. Rather, the Qualitative Pluralism seeing reality as a mixture of chemical compounds where things are only illusory, or being is the result of a biological process where all things are real, Pythagoreanism classifies thing more generically. This is useful, for how can you talk of such a general category as Being using particular issues such as Chemistry and Biology? What about Physic's? The Atomists might have a response to this. Once again, the philosophy of One is more generic than the Two. Whereas, the Atomist's hold the Universe is consistent of an infinite quantity of indivisible particles, their Theory starts to be less applicable when they throw in senses and void. Pythagoras rather reigns supreme by showing, as if to a child, that One + One = Two, One + Two = Three, and so Fourth. All things come from the One. In this sense, Pythagoras is most similar to Parmenides.

By the very fact Pythagoreanism is more generic, it is also more diverse. The Tetractys, with its interchanging of odd and even numbers, not only gives us a pictorial view of change, but it also gives us cumulative results. Each number is symbolic of certain qualities. Four represents Justice. The musical harmonies are represented in each pair of parallel lines. The point, the line, the plane and tetrahedron are in the Tetractys. The progression generates opposite alignments such as male and, if one line is skipped, female. Neither Qualitative Pluralism nor Atomism have this kind of comprehension. Both remain in a kind of stasis constantly arguing generalities when particulars are needed, and particulars when generalities are needed. By arguing for qualities, senses, the Qualitative Pluralists miss underlying laws. By arguing against qualities, and for atoms and void, the Atomists miss the qualitatively real. Neither achieves the mathematical purity of Pythagoras giving the solution to the mind and body dichotomy.

On top of this, Pythagoras introduced Dualism (in the West). Dualism is the basis of our entire Western Philosophy. By generating a system of opposites, from the Tetractys, to account for all possible things is practically self-evident. Yet, once again, this self-evident system simultaneously wraps up the metaphysical. This is a far more specific, detailed, and understandable account of being, reality, and the Universe instead of ontological arguments such as the One and the many, and atoms and void. Saying the One and the many is extremely vague, like the atoms and the void or, 'The Universe consists of porridge and berries'. Pythagoras has for more detail and accuracy. I cannot confirm what Qualitative Pluralism or Atomism are trying to say, whereas Pythagoreanism allows me to confirm the statements myself, too.

In discussing the One and the Many, the Pythagoreans achieve greater comprehension and precision of the similarities and differences in the qualitative and quantitative.

Part 04

Try as I might, I cannot see any 'problems' between On Nature and Purifications with Empedocles' notion of Immortality. Instead, I will show the coincidence between them. The only difference is the first one is scientific in purport and the second is prophetic.

The part in Purifications dealing with Immortality is Reincarnation, fragments 88-95. These are similar to fragments 1-21. Let us deal with them one by one.

Fragments 88-89, 'A daemon-goddess wraps them in a strange garment of flesh (88)... [She] took them and changed them from living creatures into dead ones (89), is identical to fragment 9, they are only worded differently. The first part of fragment 9, 'When these elements are mingled into the shape of a man living under the bright sky, or into the shape of wild beasts or plants or birds, men call it birth...' corresponds to (88). The second part, '...and when these things are separated into their parts men speak of hapless death. I follow the custom and speak as they do' is the same as (89). The difficulty is in the flow of the sentences. In fragments 88-89 it looks like Empedocles is talking about only life, when in fact he is following the same order as (9). Also, there is plenty of symbology in (88-89) causing us to miss the connection.

Fragments 90-93, 'From what high place... have I fallen (90)... In the past I have been a boy and a girl (91)... I wept and mourned (92)... We have come into this low-roofed cavern (93)' reflect the tone and discussion in 1-2 and 21. His is a lamentable mourning talking simultaneously of his own entrapment (90-92) and all others (93). We find similar discourse in 1, '…The life of mortals is so mean a thing as to be virtually un-life…' and in the beginning of fragment 2, 'Avert from my tongue the madness of such men'. Empedocles is obviously in both books discussing his misery of mortal life, something one can certainly relate to. He includes in (91) some metaphysics which relates to fragment 21. Saying he has existed in many forms is the same as in (21) when he is discussing Love and Strife: 'These alone truly are, but interpenetrating one another they become men and tribes of beasts.' The only difference, prophetic vs scientific, is Empedocles is talking about himself in one book, and many in the other.

Fragments 12-20 are the validation of the processes of the Element's and the two forces, Love and Strife. Fragments 94 and 95 are simply the natural conclusion of natural laws being applied to the individual. Whereas the first book gives the Metaphysic's, the second book gives the application. Where's the 'problem'? A key example of this is in the comparison of fragment 94, '…or has fallen into the way of Strife…' up to all of fragments 12-20. In all of fragments 12-20 the only thing Empedocles is talking about is the Element's and how Love and Strife pull them together and tear them apart. So, simply, when Empedocles is talking about 'a daemon who must walk the worlds ten thousand years', he is referring to what happens to you if you defile your Body, Mind, Spirit and Soul with blood and violence, break an oath, and most important to this discussion, what happens if you follow the way of Strife.

In essence, the two books reflect each other; one is on the personal level, the other on the universal.

Part 05

Atomism leads to its determinism by its absolute requirements for objective spatial cause. This is entirely separate from the subjective individual. This is a problem for Free Will which ultimately requires personal choice.

Leucippus sees things as a construct of surface rhythm, inter-contact, and inclination. These are respectively, shape, arrangement, and direction of turning. What allows for the motion involved in these is the void, '…he conceded to the monists that there could not be movement without a void… (T1)'. Not only that, 'Leucippus and Democritus say that all things are composed of invisible bodies, and that these are both infinite in number and shape (T3). Further in T1, 'They move in the void -for there is a void- and by their coming together they cause coming to be'.

Here is the crux. If all things are governed by a mere fluctuation of particles, and invisible to boot, then we are also governed by such. Once can then appropriately make the statement, 'Nothing happens at random; whatever comes about is by rational necessity (F1)'. That is, strict mathematical spatially quantifiable necessity. Yes sir.

By the above process the Atomist's are qualitative monists and spatial pluralists.

Democritus continues this great tradition with a personal twist. The senses are obscure Knowledge, whereas the only real Knowledge are atoms and void. This is shown in fragments 1-6. Democritus obviously puts no value on personal judgment when he says in fragment 2, 'By this criterion man must learn that he is divorced from reality'.

More fun is in fragments 10, 12, 14 and 19 which just have to be quoted here for their sheer extremity against the individual. In order, 'Do not try to understand everything lest you be ignorant of everything', 'Man is a small 'ordered world'', 'To give obedience to the law, to the ruler, and to him who is wiser than oneself, marks the well-ordered man', and totally clinical, 'Coition is a slight attack of epilepsy, in which [hu]man gushes forth from [hu]man and breaks loose with the violence of a blow'. Ow, surely, Democritus hates even the idea of a human idea.

Without question, we can now see how Atomism can lead to the cold space of Monotheistic Totalitarianism. Or are these last two words synonymous? This is, of course, Determinism. It does not create a problem for Free Will, it creates 100% unabated Hell. In this system we must obey external reality (or die), never inquire about anything, be paper copy facsimiles, and gush out our reproduction in epileptic seizure(s). In other words, do nothing, because you are incapable of doing anything; the world dictates.

By giving a purely intellectual way of looking at the world, Atomism ironically abolishes Free Will, for one would think Free Will to be caught up with the Intellect. Unfortunately, the tools we possess are our Senses in combination with our Reason. Does he put a nail into his position with fragment 8: 'Intellect: It is by convention color exists, by convention sweet, by convention bitter. Senses: Ah, wretched intellect, you get your evidence only as we give it to you, and yet you try to overthrow us. That will be your downfall.' The answer would be, Democritus by pitting the two against each other accomplishes the same letting in of Determinism and vanquishing of Free Will for Free Will cannot not exist without both.

Atomism as pure math might be stomachable. As a Humanistic Philosophy i.e. Free Will even it would prefer to roll over and die.

Part 06

To state, 'Man is the measure of all things... (F1)' is falling into an extreme position, a fault of so many. No thing is absolutely unto itself, rather a combination of variables determines something. Or better, decides something... I will refute Protagoras' contention in a variety of ways.

Let us begin with his first fragment. There is a hole in his logic. He continues (F1) as, '...of things that are, that they are; of things that are not, that they are not.' This cannot be. 'Of things that are not' is a generic existential statement. It does not say, 'Of things that are not human'. The result is, how can human who exists, be the determiner of that which does not exist? Protagoras is talking absurdity.

Next, in fragment 2, 'All matter is in a state of flux... It is our sense impressions of the thing that get modified, because affected by age and other bodily conditions.' O.K. Then, what causes our age, and our bodily conditions? Protagoras would be forced to argue, our changing impressions of the cause of our aging is what causes our fluctuating impressions. This is, of course, circulus in probando, which is bogus. There is to all things a reality independent of our perception. Most of the other Pre-Socratics, especially the Atomist's, would immediately agree to this. I could cite any one of them for back up. However, all I have to ask is, does the room cease to exist when I leave it, and why does the cat still grow hungry in its bouts of non-existence when it leaves the room? See Schrodinger's Cat Paradox.

Fragment 3, this is again circular. There are 'intelligible principles' because there are 'seemings'. These two words are hand-in-hand with perception. Effectively, it is saying Thought is because of Senses and such is a basic self-contradiction, but so what? It still tells us nothing. You cannot define Neurology with synonyms.

Fragment 4, 'Learning requires both natural endowment... It does not take root in the soul unless...' Exactly where do 'natural endowment' and 'soul' come from? Protagoras is presupposing the nature of human with a priori qualities such as soul. This cannot be done if we are the 'measure of all things' for we would discover such through Sense Data. He is contradicting himself which is bad for good learning.

Fragment 6 simply annihilates his argument, '...For the obstacles to that sort of knowledge are many, including the obscurity of the matter and the brevity of human life.' In this, he is acknowledging the existence of something called 'matter' which is blocked to us. If we were the measure of such there would be no such independent thing. And, a minor argument, we would be inextricably connected to matter, thereby removing obstacles and obscurity almost entirely. As for the argument of Reality being completely Subjective to us, which so many people get on the band wagon about, because it supports their view of Reality, Science puts a big monkey wrench into the whole deal. Through measurements we know there is quantifiable space independent of our perception i.e. there is an Absolute Zero Temperature which is specifically relative to all other temperatures and not relative to Human's with our inflated ego complex. Our varied perceptions of Space do not determine the existence, non-existence, or even the quality of that Space: The molecular structure of The Table is not modified by the perception of the Stupid Humanity. Regardless of whether I measure it with, 1, 2, 3, seconds, 4, that is what a clock is for, there is an exact real existing distance between two buildings. You can draw an infinite quantity of points on a line but that distance is still real, exact and existing.

There is also such a thing as different colors in the multi-spectrum of particles and waves throughout the Universe, and hopefully the Multiverse, too. The Atomists would have been at the Sophists throats. No thing is unto itself. Nothing does not exist. Reality is a combination of Objectivity and Subjectivity. The trick is achieving the proper relativities, a modern perspective. Now for some more fun: Nothing is the opposite of Everything, thereby affirming we cannot define anything but by its opposite...

Ionian and Italian Schools

The Ionian School consists of Thales, Anaximander and Anaximenes. The Italian School is consisted of the Pythagorean's.

Their main comparison is Rational, the usage of the Intellect to answer problems of reality. Their contrast lies primarily in the methods of Rationality. The Pythagorean's applied their minds to Nature using abstractions whereas the Milesian's described things in terms of natural phenomena.

The major similarities between these two School's are the beliefs in an infinite source to Nature and Dualism. Further, all believed in the existence of divine beings, though not as we moderns would. Divine Being's are meant as intelligent and infinite. With infinite is meant Immortal; how can you be Immortal if you can just die in a finite timeline... The other similarities are minor and are not necessarily common to all Milesian's.

The differences are more expressed as a lack in one School rather than as differing opinions of the same problem: Pythagoras taught a way of life, while the Milesian's taught a way of looking at life. The Milesian's account for the Element's while Pythagoras virtually ignores them. Last and best, the Pythagoreans concentrated on Number and Music, which is practically not heard of in the Ionian's.

To begin, the infinite, Apeiron, or one, are accountable by both School's, in different ways. This is interesting for if there is such a common agreement then it has a higher probability of being true.

Anaximander is the strongest of the Milesian's, in the expression of this, with his Apeiron from which all things come and return to. He indicates this is separate from the eternally changing flow of Element's.

Thales states this infinite living source is Water since it is evident all things have Water in them. Through a transformation process all things come from the moist seed.

Anaximenes says it is Air. Through a process of rarefaction or condensation all other Element's are formed. Air is the breath, the psuche, which is also self-evidently in all things.

Pythagoreans held the Soul is Immortal and is diffused through the entire world. The Soul is connected to the one which partakes of all things as it is considered both odd and even. Pythagoreans hold that numbers, thereby things, come out of a void, a limitless breath, so connecting in with Anaximander and Anaximenes at once. They hold the Soul to be a ratio and the Body is merely a corpse within the void which must be shed in purification to become free.

Thus, a common medium possessing the qualities of divinity or immortality is seen to exist in both the Ionian and Italian School's.

The other great connection is in concepts of opposites: Dualism. Each and every one has their version and there are overlaps.

Pythagoras' version is probably the most notable. Once again based on numbers, he formed a table of opposites represented by unlimited and limited, and odd and even, respectively. There are a total of ten pairs of which all things are supposedly constituted. Unlike the Milesians these do not create a perpetual battle field, rather 'one' is dominant or 'two' is dominant; one side of this list is on top, then the other. There is mention of it being divided as good and bad, male and female as well. It is more likely, considering his other ethical standpoints, his intentions were to be more objective. For is it not mentioned he admitted some females into his cult, and was he not married?

Thales, Anaximander and Anaximenes are all into the four Element's: Earth, Water, Air and Fire. Obviously, also the fifth, Ether played an important role. From each comes dry, wet, cold, hot, respectively, or somewhat disrespectfully, for in those they perceive duality; one cancels the other out and one sets up the other. So things are changed, created, and annihilated. As mentioned above there are different emphases. However, such a system of interacting Element's is theirs.

Though there are obviously subtleties between each School and within each School it is agreed there are such things as opposites and they are counteractive.

The Milesian's in traditional Greek sense have this notion of God's and Goddesses, though they depersonalize them. Thales states, all is blended with gods, all is ensouled with spirits and divine force. GOD is the mind in All. Anaximander gives Divinity to the Apeiron, and Anaximenes calls Air divine.

Pythagoras is god-like as well. He states, the Universe is one, intelligent, infinite, spherical, and animate. If such qualities are not divine, nothing is.

Now, I shall go onto the differences.

Pythagoras was very religious; he was not satisfied with merely observing phenomena. He had to live it. This was not done so much by the Ionian School, for one they did not set up a secret cult where one could in complete privacy amongst fellow conspirators practice all the rituals which led to divine knowledge and Divinity itself. Pythagoras had symbola, symbolic maxims, which were not just zen-like philosophical parables. They told you, 'Do not step beyond the balance point'. No, you really do not want to do that! Of course, it may be nonsense, but it went beyond abstract quips such as, 'The Earth rests upon Water'. Rather, Pythagoras had the Golden Verses. The Milesian's did not have anything like an all-encompassing system of personal conduct. Pythagoras hereby went beyond mere intellectual Philosophy and brought it to spiritual practicality, into every moment of your life, an interesting feat, if you will.

Here the Milesian's jump back. Anaximander, especially, provides a comprehensive system of elemental interaction. To them the essence of life is in the Element's. Without them, we are nothing, literally, as Anaximander shows with the Apeiron. Pythagoras rather has his neat order of numbers and explains Form as Ratio, the combination of different numbers in different degrees and geometries. To the Milesian's everything is Water, or Air, or is an interflow of Element's in the upward circle or downward circle. The very structures, forms, of matter are determined by the Element's, not these non-existent numbers.

Music and Number are paramount to Pythagoras whereas they are practically non-existent in the Ionian School. Music is a reflection of the Cosmic Order. The Planet's correspond to the harmonic intervals. These are 2:1, 3:2, 4:3, the octave, 4th, and 5th. Obviously they are more but he wanted to simplify and reduce to the universal basis of all the combinations. Whether all the rest is over redundant is still highly debatable…

It naturally follows, numbers play a big role. Accordingly, the Pythagoreans attribute number to be the Arche of the Universe, where the ratios of Music are an indicator of such. Number further is not only indicative, it is also an absolute necessity for the freeing of the soul. For without the contemplation of Order one cannot be freed. None of this is barely hinted at in the Ionian thought.

So we come full circle. The Pythagorean's introduced abstract theoretical and practical Philosophy with numbers as the central teaching and music as its main voice in the attempt to rationalize this confusing life. Meanwhile, the Milesian's chose to rationalize about Nature taking directly from the source, the Element's, in whatever proportions and emphases they come. Not per se incorrect, since technically 'void' does not exist.

It is difficult to say which of the two are more accurate or attractive and is not the subject of this essay, rather both have their appeal and we can combine the two systems. Each have very interesting comparisons and contrasts with each other and virtue unto their own. Indeed, these were fairly advanced Human Being's. What, did they see these things? They had none of our hyper modern devices in the 21st Century…

Other minor details which crop up and which are not heralded by all, or put in the foreground, are worth noting as well. At the time, the Greek World was very much in communication with the surrounding cultures. In the concept of matter and nothingness existing, and in ideas such as the void being the Arche of things, there is apparent borrowing from the Eastern Ascetic Mysticism's. Especially when they start talking of Nothingness being without beginning or end there are question marks. How many of their statements are 'original'? Pythagoras was, after all, also initiated in Babylon. Did he not simply get the whole thing from them?

Even Druid's travelled back then to get initiated in Babylon, too…

Still though, we have to find a root in the West for these things, rather than quoting Lao Tse Chung all the time… And, our language and interpretation is not the same as Vedic, Hindu, Buddhist and/or Zen-Buddhist systems, points of view, philosophies and religions.

Another interesting point is the idea of the Sphere held by Pythagoras as the One, and the Sphere held by Thales as the One, is a parallel. Also, Anaximander seeing the Earth as spherical and at the center of all things is another similarity. Of course, a good joke circulating around in intellectual elite circles is that there is no such perfect Sphere in the Universe, there are only elliptical spherical 3d objects… Thus, it could be the abstract perfect Form representing possibly the entire reality or GOD.

Also interesting is that Fire played a big role though in different parts and is ironic because that is how their culture also ended by the Goth's and Hun's. To the Pythagorean's there was a primal fire, invisible, which all of the Planet's revolved around. Anaximander saw it as a sheath surrounding the Earth, which caused the Planet's to spring into being.

In effect, these Philosopher's have a combination of serious considerations and neat childish analogies. And, once again, how could they have known what even Quantum Science is now proving if they did not see the electro-magnetic field of Planet Earth?

In conclusion, the Pythagorean's had more things in common with the Milesian's than differences. They agreed on major points, while disagreements were due to emission more so than direct conflict in similar questions. Both deserve to be recognized as the Father's Of Philosophy with their Genius of rational and intelligent thought. And all of that circa 500 B.C.!

This is still quite a challenge in a 3D Game even these days…

Timeless Aspect's

Throughout Literature there are prevailing ideas which persist over Time. These can be known as Archetypes. This essay will show through comparing the similarities of Perceval, Candide, and the The Natural how such Aspect's do exist in the Journey theme.

The similar Archetypes are as follows: Progression from Innocence to Maturity, Self-Obsession to Community Identity, The presentation of standard figures who the Adventurer encounters, Temptation/Danger, Chaos to Order, Rise and Fall, Trial/Learning, Period/Rites Of Passage. The physical, emotional, mental and spiritual Journey's are interconnected. The differences between a Normal Mortal and a Higher Mortal are shown by a measure of Pre-Destiny/Fate and Divine Intervention.

The most significant of all the Quest Archetypes is the progression of naivety to Knowledge. We can see all other Aspect's can essentially be included under this. There is a dramatic demonstration of this in all three novels. Starting with Perceval, we see Perceval's forcible kissing of the Maiden and his 'stealing' of food as primarily a product of Ignorance; his behavior was due to the unheard lessons of his Mother. From this after meeting Gornemant he achieves some lessons and thus challenges Anguingueron at another Fair Maiden's Castle for a reason; one must not harm a Maiden. Rather than causing her harm we see Perceval now preventing such. At the end of the story we are given a comparison when he comes across a decrepit Maiden. It turns out this is the First Maiden and so as to eliminate the Injustice being done to her he soundly beats the Proud Knight after acknowledging his role in her plight. Thus we see him developing a Code Of Honor from a state of blundering.

In Candide, about 500 years later, the same occurs in different words. Candide after reacting from mere urge gets kicked out of Paradise for kissing Cunegonde, the most Fair Maiden ever. He gets used by everybody and their dog. Then he meets her again. Then he loses her again. At this point he makes the decision to do nothing else except find her and marry her with all the gold he has from Eldorado. So his life is gaining a Focus. After losing almost all the gold he finally comes to the conclusion of the temporality of material wealth and comes up with the maxim, 'I also know that we must cultivate our garden'. He also does this with a disfigured Cunegonde. They live happily ever after.

Another 500 years later and we are in our century in America. So nothing better than to show Roy's blind drive to be the best in Baseball without him comprehending any of the realities such as the Politic's involved in the game. Resulting, he gets shot. When he returns he is shafted on the bench for months because of Bump and his unwillingness to go to 'Psych Prep' meetings.

He makes the decision to tough it out. Now he is only out in left field... At the end, the bloody end, he is forced to battle his instinctive line drives for Memo against a purely moral decision of selling out. He succeeds at the final out in the final World Series game to decide against selling out. He is too far in though and can only hit a killer foul ball which is almost a homerun.

Pre-occupation with Self to World or Community Awareness is very obvious in all. Perceval wants nothing else but to be a Knight, after thinking, due to their shining armoré and noble builds that they are Angel's. Later, or rather throughout, we observe him sending one Knight after another to Arthur's Court for their wrong deeds. So he is a Bringer of Truth which demands consciousness of world relativities; he distinguishes between Good and Evil.

Candide first wants nothing more than his Survival, then nothing more than Cunegonde. After discovering 'the world is full of evils' from his whole trek he has satisfied his philosophical yearnings and settles down. Thus he has achieved his societal position.

There is incredibly strong ambition in Roy: His life is worthless unless he is Number One in Baseball. He succeeds. Unfortunately it does not last and he is forced to see the harsh and brutal reality around him. The pinnacle of this is the ending where a young Kid asks him about selling out, 'Say it ain't true Roy.' At this point he knows as another Lady said, 'He coulda been a King.' Painful, yet true it is.

Each Protagonist encounters similar figures. They meet Antagonist's, Enemy's, Benefactor's, Mentor's, Virgin Maiden's, Temptresses, True Lover's, Father Figures, Mother Figures and not necessarily in that order. A comparison of Virgin Maiden's, Temptresses, and Mentor's will be given.

Perceval possibly has the most account of these. In fact he hardly knows which is which. In this regard such figures are relative to him. The Proud Knight's Lady in her tent, on her own, the first Lady he meets, is to him a Virgin Maiden, bestowed with her inequitable charm, is first to touch his heart. Then in the besieged Castle is a Temptress who he fights for who wants a Husband for her Castle. Gornement is his Mentor teaching him the stirrups and the Lance and not to constantly refer to his Mother.

Candide is lucky for his Virgin Maiden ends up being his True Love though in slightly altered Form. For that one fatal First Kiss his whole life begins. As it turns out, he is lucky again, for there being only one Woman in his life, she is also his Temptress. And woe the trouble she brings him to. Candide has two Mentor's. One is Pangloss who taught him Optimism and started him off in Philosophy. The other is Martin, a Pessimist, who is with him most of his Hell Ride and at the end.

Roy is also besotted with others. Before he is shot, on his way to be signed, he has his first touch of a girl named Harriet. Memo is an endless Temptress for him. He is ultimately doomed by her. A Mentor, though also a Virgin Maiden, is Iris. She redeems him in two, though related, completely different ways.

As can be seen, Temptation/Danger plays a large Role in all these novels. Conflict after all is the basis of all stories. In general, Perceval searches it out, it searches Candide out, and Roy is not aware it is looming always just behind him...

In a similar vein these Journey's progress from a complicated random Play, both in the Protagonist's and in their World's, to achieved and resplendent Order. This is shown in Perceval's decisions, at first reactive, then based on Code Of Honor. Candide is thrown into the snow, beat repetitively, wanders aimlessly, then he starts choosing where to go. Resulting, he eventually achieves an ordered Home. Roy is thrown into Chaos with a silver bullet and he is brought to Order by his Fate being thrown unceremoniously back into his hands: Sell out or starve.

So the Cycle of Rise and Fall gets its turn. Perceval has a chance to be wedded and running his very own Castle. Instead, he ends with a Hermit. Candide achieves more riches than he could possibly imagine and ends being a Farmer. Roy, most obviously, rises to total Fame, and ends as a Bum in the gutter.

Throughout all of this there are steps, Door's which each must pass through. These Rites Of Passage are fundamental to any Journey. These essentially teach the Hero. Perceval learns from the Fisher King to know what one should do, appropriately, in specific Scenario's. Though it is not his fault he still learns from his Innocent error and can prevent future doom to the land. Candide, at heart optimistic, learns to temper his childish enthusiasm by balancing it with Reality. Roy learns the hard way. He is crushed to the core in his lesson of not pursuing the image of the 'Perfect Female'. He is shown what is deeper.

The Journey's are not just in this World. Perceval's Quest for The Grail is a travelling through Wood's, Plain's, Hill's where reside Monster's and Evil Knight's. It is a pursuit for personal emotional satisfaction from trouncing Monster's and Evil Knight's and making it through the terrain to return to his Mother and ultimately, spiritually, to restore himself to Purity and cleanse his wrong doings by finding The Grail. As is shown here all three depend on one another. In Candide the cross-overs are with his Trek all over the Earth, to return to Cunegonde, to answer his Philosophical Question of Optimism. They all occur simultaneously and depend on each other. Roy goes to the Ball Park to make it big, win Memo, and fulfill a Life Goal. Not only are all at the same place, they are blurred into one another.

To place their Character's over and above the Common Mortal they give credence to Fate and sometimes utilize Divine Intervention itself. One example of each is as follows: Perceval is a Natural. He does not need to learn his tools. Divine Intervention would be his hypnosis by the blood in the snow so King Arthur's troupe can find him. Candide's life is divinely intervened on by the King Of The Bulgarian's at the beginning. Pre-Destiny is shown in his remarkable ability to survive all these near Death's, as on the ship with the Anabaptist and in the earthquake City with Martin. Roy is also a born Natural. Iris can also be seen as a pseudo Supernatural Intervention to stop a crucial slump of his. Often the distinction between Natural and Supernatural is absent.

It can be seen in Perceval, Candide, and The Natural, the existence of Common Element's. These Archetypal Themes in Literature are Timeless because each of these stories are separated by 500 years. In a 2000 year period there are many, in some cases identical, similarities. Only the Form's have changed.

Searle and the Churchland's

There is a fundamental difference between the Mind and Computer Program's. Searle provides the argument in support of this. His main stance is the distinction between meaning and laws, content and form, or semantics and syntax. He also provides the alternative related explanation for the Mind-Body Interaction which turns out to be his defense of Materialism: The brain causes mental states and processes. I will clarify his successful arguments and add a few points myself.

Let us begin with the basis of Searle's argument (see pg. 134 Beta) and its reply. We will show its ineffability:

1. Computer Program's are formal (syntactic).
2. Human Mind's have mental contents (semantics).
3. Syntax by itself is neither constitutive of nor sufficient for semantics.

Its strongest reply (so far) is by the Churchlands (pp. 140 and 142). Note the Churchlands parallel construction:

1. Electricity and Magnetism are forces.
2. The essential property of Light is luminance.
3. Forces by themselves are neither constitutive of nor sufficient for Light.

By themselves these arguments, respectively The Chinese Room and The Luminous Room seem a little vague and pretentious. One can say they are presumptuous in their claims merely setting up appropriate antecedents for their conclusions.

However, let us point out their method. By generating two true statements which are opposite one can draw a few conclusions from that comparison. This is Liebniz's Law #1: 'One and the same thing cannot both have a property and its opposite'.

Thus, we must explore each of the points. If either is proven wrong then the other is true. Let us also see if the claims in each argument are actually opposite i.e. is semantics opposite to syntax?

Are computers formal? What is formal? Formal is defined in Philosophy as... This is a good question: What does Philosophy define things as? Let us look at the Webster Dictionary. Under 'formal logic' we see 'the branch of logic that studies the validity or correctness of conclusions by investigation of their structural relation to other propositions as evidence'. Good thing we have a University Education otherwise we would not be able to understand that sentence and the rest of our time would be spent decoding it... We will presume you have already done that. Since we are talking Philosophy, we have discovered (by accident) a more useful definition under the word 'form': 'The ideal nature or essential character of a thing as distinguished from its matter'. Good, now we have something. Now we can start. The purpose of this lengthy description is to indicate the importance of definition, especially in Philosophy. See also The Free Show which I have finished defining version 3 of in 2010, version 4.4 is also done now. As my Uncle also said, Ir. W.I.J. Lans R.I.P., '...if you do not first define your principles then you have no clue what you're talking about...' In addition, if you do not know what Syntax is (now you do), how could you know what its opposite is?

Thus, Syntax is formal, for the above described method is exactly how Computer's work. They utilize digital electronics, the 'formal' manipulation of 'symbols', such as bits, 0's and 1's, to work. Input comes streaming in, a particular pattern of electricity through switches, which is coded through various levels in the operating system, 0's and 1's up to the user interface, which the programs reads and translates into our Human Language, and based on the particular order of bits of data a particular output is generated. Without question Computer's are syntactical, but the Noobie or a Standard User using the thing is not, for who would question the formal nature of this process? And, as another good joke, my late Uncle also said you can technically run the thing with chocolate milk...

Does the Mind involve semantics? Yes, let us look up semantics. Webster tells us semantics: '(is) the branch of linguistics concerned with the nature, structure, and, esp., the development and changes, of the meanings of speech forms, or with contextual meaning'. The key word there for those of us who know the subjective indicative is 'meanings'. We will presume you know what 'meaning' means... hmmm... no wonder this Backwater Colony Planet...

Thus, one would definitely say, by applying that sentence to our Mind, that yes, we have such things as comparative definitions which interrelate. In other words, we know the difference between an Apple and an Orange and can apply a name to each and provide multiple examples of their usages. Like peeling off layers... pfff... Without definition there is no meaning. Since we know our Mind's are capable of this we know our Mind's have semantics.

Do Noobie Mind's have syntax? When I look at all our emotions back then and now...

So, ou est la difference? The semantical definition even used the word 'form' in it and 'contextual' immediately brings structure to Mind. The syntactical definition sounds like a comparison of meanings, for without structural relation how can you have meaning?

This is the argument the Churchland's used. They do not consider there to be a difference (see pp. 142 last paragraph to 144). They agree the serial machine, and serial worker, symbol manipulating Computer does not sufficiently account for Consciousness. However, they think with the advent of more sophisticated devices, such as Parallel Processing Devices, and possibly even more tactile versions which incorporate different substances other than neurochemicals in different hardware other than a cat's eyeball, which essentially perform the same way, which can read and respond to their environment, that such a replication rather than just a simulation will be possible. And again, as my Uncle liked to say, your sense of smell is only a chemical reaction, however what about our feeling of it, a qualitative value?

We can rely on Science to verify their three points. Are Electricity and Magnetism forces? What is a force? In Webster's: '(Physic's) The cause, or agent, that puts an object at rest, into motion or alters the motion of a moving object'. Electricity is (I will take the easiest one): 'electric current supplied as a public utility for lighting, heating, etc...' Does Light or heat move? We see: '...heat is considered a form of energy whose effect is produced by the accelerated vibration of molecules...' Bingo, we have shown without doubt, that Noobie's vibrate hard, that Churchland's axiom one is true.

Is the essential property of Light luminance? The definition is: 'The form of electromagnetic radiation that acts upon the retina of the eye...' This should be sufficient to indicate its essence is Light for we know our eyes work with Light.

Therefore, just like Searle says, we put two true statements together, and we draw a third which is true. So, Electricity and Magnetism are neither constitutive of nor sufficient for luminance. Except there is one problem: That is not a true statement. So, Churchland is laughing in his clever miming of Searle and Searle is had. Retort: 'Wrong again Churchland!'

What went wrong though? To quote Searle (pg. 137 last paragraph): 'The account of light in terms of electromagnetic radiation is a causal account right down to the ground'. In other words, the Churchlands' analogy is incorrect, or it is not an analogy. Searle's two statements are opposite to one another obeying Liebniz. The Churchlands' statements are causal. Such is a slight difference...

Now we can ask the pressing question, 'Is syntax opposite to semantics?', for if it is not, Searle's argument goes down the tube.

This is a difficult question to say the least. What are all the fine details determining whether one thing is opposite to another? In Literature we do not have the precision of Algebra where we can say when two triangles have one 90° angle each, we know their other two angles are equal. Language is extremely varied and its usage is far from universal. Oh, what one would give for a universal definition... You may have noticed for every word in the dictionary, excluding technical terms, there are at least several, 3-4, definitions.

This is why German, English, Dutch and French are strong Contextual Objective Languages. This is also why we get to you use capitals, again, to define Object's.

It is best, unless we want to go into a 4000 page book to leave this argument at this point. Let us be content with, and hopefully the reader will, with my attempt to indicate in which direction the answer lies. Whereas the writer dislikes doing this, nothing can be done about it with the present laws of the English Language and the present state of Philosophy in general. Which if we look at the necessity for Unique Values and the avoidance of Double Definitions, especially in Information Technology, it is just atrocious. IT at least comes out a little better if you program it correctly and returns an Error if you hit a Non-Unique Value but most do not causing massive system failures.

Also, the huge difference which I have learned in my 19 years of experience living in The Hague, 6 months before in Amsterdam, between Listening, Reading, Writing and Speaking makes it impossible to make any form of universal or absolute definition. What is still interesting to me is that Dutch is actually 10 times harder to speak than the other ones which makes me sound like a Noobie and affects my job potential badly; I can't even do Sales here because of such. In summitry a repeat simplification of this entire debate rests on this question: 'Is semantics opposite to syntax?' If not, we have an entirely new playing field…

With the strongest argument of the Churchland's dealt with we can turn our attention to a few of the minor arguments. Most of Searle's disclaimers rest on the idea of formal structures versus content. Just like Google, 'Content drives the media…'

The Systems Reply (pg. 122) is the most absurd, as though a room could have Consciousness. It tries to indicate the relative meaninglessness of the individual regardless of where the individual is. This kind of blatant Hegelism is not even obviously said. Searle is clever in response and tells them to go internalize the Chinese symbols into the individual's brain where he is seeing them. The result is, since there is nothing actually separate from the individual(s) and the room, the process is still meaningless regardless of where the room is.

The Robot Reply (pg. 124) is an off-spin of basic Pavlovian and Skinnerian Behaviorism; everything the individual is is because of conditioning. As Functionalism shows, however, there is a lot more happening inside the Black Box than just input and output indicates. As Searle says (pg. 125), 'Now in this case I want to say that the robot has no intentional states at all; it is simply moving about as a result of its electrical wiring'. To describe Consciousness by external variables is not only a contradiction, it is also the epitome of superficialness expialidotious.

The Brain Simulator Reply is showing the whole direction this argument is going; it relies on Materialism. The problem with it is stated in its title. The best one can achieve by simulating the brain, our neural network is exactly that, a simulation. Searle repeats again (pg. 125, 2nd last paragraph), 'As long as it simulates only the formal structure of the sequence of neuron firings at the synapses, it won't have simulated what matters about the brain, namely its causal properties, its ability to produce intentional states'. I think it is good to interject here that an intellectual mathematical isolated Theory cannot account for the interactivity of our minds with our external environment. Ours is a biological mechanism using stimuli, not just the geometry of our neurons. Consciousness may very well be due to our environment as well.

The Combination Reply (pg. 125) is a compilation of the previous three. Searle gives it more than we would, forming the basis for real qualitative value, not just only quantitative, in his position. Searle does not disagree with the potential for a Consciousness Replicating Machine provided they have the same causal powers as brains (pg. 130, last paragraph). If the combination generates this then fine it works, however he says (pg. 126, 1st paragraph), '…the only real locus of intentionality is the (hu)man'. In any case, how can one prove or disprove this argument? Space is not the final frontier, it is your brain…

The Other Minds Reply (pg. 126) cannot hope to work for it evades the question, saying we can only know people's behavior not their cognition. Searle is more generous saying the question is not how we know cognition, rather it is what cognition is; do not 'feign anesthesia' (pg. 127).

The Many Mansions reply is similar to Churchland and proposes that Artificial Intelligence (AI) is about more than just digital and analog computers. If the Technology improves we could replicate the causal powers of the brain. Searle agrees, if that is the thesis. Searle is arguing against the original thesis: 'mental processes are computational processes over formally defined elements' (pg. 127).

Here we come to the climax of the issue. The Mind is the Program to the brain, the hardware. No, it is not. This is because a pre-fixed system of hardware and software is insufficient for our fluctuating internal and external dependent Intentionality. Or, Free Will. Rather, the Mind is a serial or parallel process over a parallel brain (unless you take serotonin inhibiting drugs like LSD); the brain also causes the Mind for it has to work stimuli. Thus, the heavy focus on Biological Psychology and Psychiatry these days, in fact it is so bad that Psychology has been almost completely replaced by Psychiatry, there are no more Pep Talk's, Cries On A Shoulder, deep analytical solutions presented by Freud and Jung, including exploration of sub-conscious and Lucid Dream's, it has become one big Pill Society with rising Hellth Cost's...

This, of course, is potentially disastrous and is proven as to why Addict's, like myself to Cigarettes, Sjek, Marijuana and Alchohol have a 9 out of 10 recurring statistical rate and are never cured; there are no accounts for my perception, interpretations, feelings, emotions and reactions; MRI Scan's are just beginning but are bloody expensive and are done with live reaction to stimuli: You still need an interpreter.

Thus, the analogy of Computer to Brain is false, for no software and/or hardware caused the existence of any software and/or hardware of my Intentional Consciousness, or Free Will. It most certainly does not account for all the other qualitative experiences such as my feelings and emotions; what computer screen shows anymore but a neural electrical spike in activity on a graph?

I can easily back this up with many arguments, primarily, if I choose to just turn left in my auto and drive straight into a store window then that is my prerogative.

In conclusion, based on above logic, reason, arguments, evidence (proof?) one can also not with any certainty state as to whether content is opposite to layout, syntax opposite semantics, it is more like they are hand-in-hand and cannot function without each other's existence. Each function and program has its focus and specialty which is why I avoid all of that Camp Playing which is predominant in the entire History Of Humanity. Do I also have to be a Walking Advertisement for your big machine?

From the Local Function to the Global Function, if we do not all work better together than the World in the Universe will not develop in the correct direction and as we see in the beginning of the 21st Century on many news channels there are many calamities.

BIBLIOGRAPHY Churchland P.M., Churchland P.S., Could a Machine Think? Classical AI is unlikely to yield conscious machines; systems that mimic the brain might, Scientific American: 'Artificial Intelligence: A Debate', Jan. 1990, Vol. 262, #1. Nelson, Foster, and Scott, Webster New World Dictionary, The World Publishing Company, 2nd College Edition, Complete Reference Edition, 1970. Searle J.R., Is the Brain's Mind a Computer Program? No. A program merely manipulates symbols whereas a brain attaches meaning to them, Scientific American: 'Artificial Intelligence: A Debate', Jan. 1990, Vol. 262, #1. Searle J.R., Minds, Brains and Programs, MIT Press, Bradford Books, sixth printing, 1988.

Breaking The Speed Of Light Is Not Impossible With Null EM Field's

Part 01

I will first describe and define some relevant topics leading the other parts.

1. If the Degree Of Severity does not equal the Degree Of Severity then it generates more Karma.
2. If the result of the resolving of Degree Of Severity of Karma does not result in 0 or 1 then it generates more Karma.
3. Karma is therefore a Quantum Equation at near-infinite cross referenced variables = 0 or 1

Making the actual Mathematical Quantum Equation is better left to such experts but I imagine one of the simplest is the standard:
$$(2A + 3B + 4C) \times (5D) = 0 \text{ or } 1.$$

This is not impossible.

However, what I am proposing is that Karma actual utilizes a whole range of such equations to satisfy each Type Of Karma.

Therefore, also at Near-Infinite and Infinite for Karma is not limited to the Material Plane Of Existence only.

Part 02

Dimension's are no more than the 3D spherical bound realities within One Big Reality with the actual number of points in odd or even, asymmetrical or symmetrical Form's, respectively.

Example: For String Theory the 13th Hell Dimension is simply within and without the near-infinite Universe and infinite Reality.

They all overlap though you may be stuck in that one…

You are then in that Timeline which the 1-Nth Dimension, possibly reduced to 1-20th Dimension's, a Plane Of Existence, is more like the inclination of the entire Solar System within the Celestial Constellation 3D Grid, bound by the laws of those numbers as laid down by not only

Judaism, but the Pythagorean's, Druid's, Islam and Christianity. Each, of course, has a slightly different interpretation.

Now, Quantum Science and the String Theory are catching up and rewriting the lost and/or secret formulas.

Hopefully, Philosophy shall gain some ground, too, for hardly any High School's or Post-Education Institutes even offer Philosophy...

Part 03

'Would that be you're missing the whole gate?' says Silver, High Wizard.

'The clue has to be in Gate Technology, how else do we get there near-instantaneously?' says Silber, Psionic Warlock.

'Otherwise, a very long time, thru wormy hole curving, not angular, thru spacy wacy...' says Mr. Newbie, Rules Lawyer.

'You will not find the portal in the light but in the shadows, look at the spaces in between, where do you think all the black is coming from...' says Revlis, Vampire Demon.

Thus, to repeat, in my Poetry Lore it states, 'How to make a step before a step is learned...'

'Is it low or hi-res polygons...?!' says Revlis, Vampire Demon.

'Well, nuthin' like the Explorer, get there, many die tryin', and send a signal back at Near-Absolute Zero Mass and if you live then we have our Space Colony.' says Silber, Psionic Warlock.

To be inspired by Tolkien, too:

'It is one stone which carries them all.

It is one ring which binds them all.

It is one idea which leads them all.'

Part 04

Center of Space = 0. 1 vertex out = 1. A line = 2. Squares next to each other = 4. Hexagon's next to each other = 6. However, octagons next to each don't line up together to form a perfectly seamed 2D or 3D terrain...

Thus Space Time is not perfectly symmetrical unless the result is a Perfect Sphere. There are many unaccounted for 'spaces in between'. Mixing squares, hexagons and octagons together breaks down eventually: Try it on a piece of paper using 2D or 3D geometrical forms.

Time or a Timeline goes along and through these 2D and 3D vertexes and objects which shows that it is curved due to the path combinations from Point A to Point B. This also applies in concordance with 10, 12, 14,16 and so forth. Odd numbers lead to peculiar shapes with even more holes. 3's line up neatly as triangles ad infinitum but it quickly breaks down and we cannot draw a 'whole space'.

Flowers follow these patterns and fractal laws also show this.

To travel through Space Time at Speed Of Light (and faster) we have to follow the vertexes along and through the spaces of the 2D or 3D geometrical shapes.

Also to Null Teleport through the 2D Grid or 3D Grid… then only map and Mass Effect problem. See Conversion of Matter to Energy in many Science Field's.

All shapes and objects come from spaces and vertexes forming geometrical objects on the 2D or 3D+ dimensions and planes in the material Plane Of existence and non-material Planes Of Existence in Space Time.

Timeline = Straight or Curved Vertice along vertices or through spaces. All of these 2D or 3D Grid's overlap each other in the Universe. Do Multiverses overlap each other? See Black Holes by primarily Stephen Hawking.

Space is between the connected 2D or 3D points of the matter object which is primarily hollow. To repeat, though the zero-point-field theory does not allow empty space it does not state anything about outside of the Universe.

Thus, the cardinal 6 directions are hard to beat for how does one place the 2D or 3D polygons next to each other in perfect symmetry?

In concordance with the necessity of travelling through them in s-lines we see a perfectly straight line practically does not exist in Reality. Why not in symmetry 8, 10, 12, 14, 16 also…

We can apply this to computers too such as 32 bits and does this have potential for 2D and the future of 3D quantum circuit boards in computers?

'12 directions is not enough for Space Combat, that is why the Russian's and Chinese and Japanese are beating us…' says Silber, Psionic Warlock (Marine, Jet Fighter Pilot, Space Combat Pilot).

24 directions is therefore exactly double the 2D Hexagon and 3D Hexa-cube which is a Helical Geometrical Form.

48, 36, 24 and 12 in Numerology supported by Religion's, Philosophy and Sciences are the numbers of day and night in clock. Thus, a full circle it is.

Due to necessity of shapes in proximity with vertices and spaces we cannot access pure fluidic space in a matter object unless we can make it Near-Massless. However, it is still highly dubious as to whether we can break free from the constructs of Space Time itself, especially not in some Space Ship.

We bound by the Lines Of Time or Timelines (straight or curved vertices) and the near-infinite quantity and quality of 2D or 3D Geometrical Shapes or Form's symmetrically and asymmetrically in relation to each other.

To go beyond Light Speed or Speed Of Light one needs to reduce Mass of Object to near-nihil and Null Planar Teleport through vertices but we have no Space Grid Map of the Universe let alone other dimensions.

Part 05

The constant of Time in C^2 in Einstein's Relativity Theory is highly relative…

If you simply remove Time or it is not a constant then the result = Infinity = Insta Travel.

However, we are still limited by the medium. What is faster than the medium of Light?

Einstein stated that an Object with Mass is limited by Light Speed. Did he state how much Mass?

Now, Science has discovered a Type of Light Foton with practically Zero Mass which near-instantaneously blasts across the Universe.

Yet, something which exists still has to have some Mass.

Zero Mass = Nothing. QED.

Thus, like Infinite Absolute Zero Temperature which you can never reach cause it does not exist Near-Absolute Zero Mass must result in Hyper Light Speed.

QER: An Object with Zero Mass does not exist.

At least in the Material Plane Of Existence…

Yet, we cannot for all purposes exit the Universe. And who would argue Information, Mind and Spirit and Soul? Science is highly limited by Body. We keep thinking we have to physically get there. See Evolutionary Essays of mine at Silverlingo.com or Planesofexistence.eu and published by AuthorHouse UK where I state the following: Matter => Energy => Information => Spirit => Soul. Thus, meaning it is theoretically not impossible with the Transformation and Law of Conservation of Energy to kill Mass.

However, that is like saying I need to enter the Higher Spirit Plane in the After Life to explore the whole Universe which would otherwise at only Speed Of Light take 1000's of years rather than the necessity of Space Colonization in years and decades.

'So, we are missing somethin'…' says Silver, High Wizard.

'Next to the Space Ship, of course…' says Silber, Psionic Warlock.

Part 06

Near-Infinite or Infinite Energy or Null Potentialus Ad Majorus can be described by raising a pebble to the top of the Universe and dropping it and letting it be pulled by the central EM Force of the Universe to near-infinite speeds. The resulting Kinetic Energy through the Newton and Maxwell Theory is Near-Infinite, or is it Infinite in the Multiverse Theory?

Therefore an Object at Near-Zero Mass as a direct proportion to Zero Mass, decides how fast the Object can travel beyond the Speed Of Light for Einstein is stuck in his system with his constant.

Time is not constant; if we remove the constant or give it other values then it breaks the Speed Of Light.

Speed Of Light is a constant but that states that such is the final medium. We are now discovering the Shadow Medium and as described above there are many holes in space. There is Dark Energy and Dark Matter and this accounts for the majority of the Universe as recently discovered in Quantum Science. These are whole fields where stars cluster together more densely like a glue or membrane of the Universe: See Through The Wormhole With Morgan Freeman. If we had a means of rematerializing through such a transformation process like in Star Trek then there is also no limit except the distance of the signal.

This is actually not original since there is nothing original in Infinity.

I hope this will provide a supporting position to other paragraphs on Internet and strengthen our position, for it is crucial to Gate Technology, and the complete absurdity it would take 1000's of years just to send a probe through the Near-Infinite Material Universe. Presently it takes years and decades with Fossil Fuel's, also ridiculous by weight alone, to explore another Planet. Ion Drives are in the making which utilize the particles and waves in EM Field's but that still doesn't change the distance to get out of the Solar System. So to be poetic again, 'Do we first have to get there to get there…'

The Universe in the Material Plane Of Existence being Near-Infinite is not the Multiverse and/or the One Big Reality being Infinite.

Infinite ≠ Near-Infinite.

Immortality is therefore not being limited to the material body in the Near-Infinite Universe but rather the progression of the Spirit from the Universe, to the Multiverse to somehow the One Big Reality.

The Spirit also being Near-Massless approaching Zero Mass ad infinitum is also not limited by the Speed Of Light and can theoretically even Null Planar Teleport to another Solar System in another Galaxy where it could potentially reincarnate in the womb of another Species to be freed or doomed.

As to whether the Spirit, or even the Soul, needs to become one with all the numerological bipolar opposite hierarchies as purported in most Religion's and many Philosophy's plus some Sciences or escape in Escapism which is so popular these days from the host body vessel is still highly debatable. Rather, it seems that such are sheaths on the material Body, or layers, for when we die we do not weigh the same. Does this mean Spirit or Soul still have Mass? Yes, to repeat, or they do not exist.

Maybe, it is another case of Both, the 02 binary which Quantum Computer's are just starting on though it seems to cause a Logic Bomb in our system of opposites and 0's and 1's for how can two statements both be true? Boolean Logic spits that out.

Conclusion

Thus, like the 3D Game Mass Effect and Newton and Maxwell's Theory the best theory is to reduce the Mass of the Object to Near-Zero by negating the effects of the EM Field's ruling Gravity in the entire Universe. Then we should be able to whip along rather than just bobble like a Renaissance Galleon.

This could theoretically be done by increasing the strength of the Null EM Shield And Sphere so it pushes out the otherwise overlapping EM Field's.

By then changing the polarity, the EM Field of Planet Earth does this regularily, you can generate 360° maneuvarable Null EM Propulsion Engines and break the Speed Of Light.

Not if it is a massive Elite Colony Spaceship though, then it would be torn apart, like storm and gales on the ocean.

Is Our Reality Mind Or Body Or Subjective Or Objective?

The various fields have been touting about the question of Mind vs Body for centuries, especially since Descartes. The problem is outdated; anything several centuries old these days becomes rapidly archaic. The result is a variety of theories such as Computationalism, Functionalism, Connectionism, Representationalism, Materialism, Physicalism, Reductionism, Idealism, Mentalism, Intentionalism, ad hoc.

Computationalism and Functionalism are a little more interesting in that they avoid usual Mind or Body stances. Unfortunately, these two are a little inhuman. Here, we are proposing the motion beyond Dualism. We would choose Computationalism and/or Functionalism, however what would happen to all the Phenomenologists such as Nagel? One question remains with the discarding (or 'Descarting') of the excessively annoying and extremely debated Mind/Body dichotomy. This is the question of, 'Is our reality subjective or objective?' If this is toted around as much as the other we might actually get somewhere. The preferable position to take on this question is multi-leveled. There exists an Objective Plane, separate from our Subjective Scope. Plato supports this, too.

Since the writers Gardner, Boden, Feldman, Chomsky, Ross, Nagel and Searle also touch on this we will grab a few gems from their midst.

Gardner talks about the Subjective. They are Subjective suggesting we merely have to 'bring innate knowledge to conscious awareness' (pg. 3 Beta). The fall into a standard trap in this labyrinth is unavoidable. By bringing up a postulate that cannot be proven is granting incompetency; one cannot shed light on the innate, it is too far in shadow.

Boden is all for Computationalism. In 'Promise And Achievement in Cognitive Science' she is full of witty remarks and gay style over how much potential Computationalism has: '…it promised to illuminate the whole of Psychology: Human and animal, individual and social, normal and abnormal, cognitive and motivational, perceptual and motor -not forgetting personality, madness, and hypnosis' (pg. 8). Heady stuff, indeed! She is certainly aiming for the multiple instantiation and multiple level approaches like we are. She sees how the structure, form, body, or brain is the computer for the program or content, matter, mind. The trouble is, she does not consider our premise too much. If all of those are seen as Subjective vs Objective her whole position deteriorates. This is true because Computationalism, a mere Software/Hardware analogy, a symbol binary manipulation, cannot account for the subtleties of each of our personal experiences let alone the entire reality. What is human and animal in the schema of things? And so on down the line.

Feldman attempts to battle Boden, fairly well. And, sry (!), her statement (pg. 30), '…there are aspects of human experience that are fundamentally different for the person having them and for the scientific observer' falls just short. Her trouble is her terminology. By using ambiguous terms and Mind/Body terms she moves a lot of chains around but does not break free. The aspects are not different for the person and the scientist. Considered as a 4th person point of view both are Subjective. What is so Objective about a Scientist? What is so Objective about their tools? Their tools are human-made for Human Senses! And, recently they have shown theoretically that the Observer is a part of and can modify the experiment. In the Universal sense her comparison does not hold up.

Chomsky is distinctly Objective. He progresses his essay through various stages to its pinnacle: The rule system for language. He even gives us some particular comments on sentences which are partially accurate. Language use, acquisition, and learning are done via a Rule System. Before this is set up, it was habits, dispositions, and conditioning, Subjective things, not an Objective Rule System. Regardless of his stance, even the Modular Theory of a fixed switchbox central to a network of pathways triggered by a finite number of switches is flawed, Chomsky is missing one of the components. In one he is ignoring the Objective Reality, in the other he is missing the personal relevance and application. The Modular Theory attempts to be Objective and so ignores the human being.

Ross questions the whole field, which is encouraged. The question though is how can you try to say the subject matter of the Mind does not exist? See pg. 46. He goes about this subtly, we are sure, probably to avoid artillery fire. You cannot fool anyone into believing they do not have something in their brain. He also criticizes advanced Philosopher's and Psychologist's (last paragraph). This is not nice though we all do it. How is one to study a field, subjectively or objectively, without advanced practitioners? His criticisms are misplaced.

So, Nagel asks about that 'something'. His is a fine exposition on the existence of Consciousness. For the particulars though it is hard to agree. Up to pg. 59 is a lot of arguments for the futility of the human condition, in its unavoidable Subjectivity. After this is a failed attempt to satisfy his question with Physicalism. He rounds up with 'a speculative proposal' (pg. 62) which comes near ours. Asking the question is like begging the question. All Nagel accomplishes is a rehashing of the Mind/Body Syndrome and a confirmation of the existence of a Consciousness in a Creature. But, Nagel, we know that.

Finally, great guns, Searle comes along again. No longer do we doubt the validity of Cognitive Computational Science. Of course, the human is more complex! Symbol manipulation in a program does not reflect the experiential moment. Syntax is not intrinsic to Physic's! It is relative to the Observer. 'But that is the end of the story' (pg. 85). He stops there. It was just getting good. Instead, he develops a 4-step program which is summed up in 8 steps (neat trick that) and completely misses the crucial experiment of his 'observer relative' comments. Searle's emphases, negative or positive, on Computationalism leads him astray. The question is as crucial as the answer, and the questions on pg. 72, relating Brain/Mind to Computer is biased. Most importantly he, like all the others, has the Mind/Body reference, rather than the Subjective/Objective reference.

Rather than a Dualistic position which any discussion of Mind/Body results in, a multi-leveled gradational approach is necessary. This addresses the problem properly. We can then do formulized experiments to compare and contrast Subjective Reality's with Objective Reality in a per sector module based system to see if there are any corollaries. Through this we will eventually reduce the variables and eliminate falsities. In this system, Mind and Body take their turns in the Subjective realms, Objective realms, and through all the degrees i.e. Collective Consciousness as being more Objective than the Human Mind or Body.

One good thing to point out, however, with the advent of Biological Psychiatry dominance in the beginning of the 21st Century is the question of how much of the Mind being directly connected to the brain is not actually Body, millions of neurons and synapses giving various sensations…

Without doubt there exist Degrees Of Reality, not per se only Duality's. This phenomenon can be understood by analyzing the human condition and the Universe, in the Universe, resulting the likely probability that Mind and Body are not opposite of each other, rather Aristotle flows neatly upward into Plato flowing downwards.

In most cases, not excluding my own, somewhat not neatly leading to Sickness And Disease World again…

Falsity Of Reductionist Biological Psychiatry

Saying Reductionist Biological Psychiatry is referring to mental states and/or processes being primarily disposed to non-mental states and/or processes. These involve the ignoring of mental references. The fields which hold the view are the Behaviorist's, Materialist's, and Functionalist's. Behaviorist's are the most blatant with this, Materialist's are Reductionist's in terms of type/type identities, and Functionalist's are more general and systematic. A method of Reductionism is bound to fail for it ignores and/or over-complicates a component of the Mind Body Problem: The Mind.

Behaviorist's with the banner of Skinner focus on inputs and outputs of system. With Descarte's influence we were introduced to the concept of the reflex arc, the correlation between an event, stimulus, to a response, behavior. With Pavlov's Classical and Operant Conditioning the interaction of this methodology was expounded. Essentially, what all of these theorists are attempting to do, and modern Behaviorist's, is base Cognitive Science on observable events only.

Observable only then logically implies *only* physical; only that which is tangible can be noticeable. The philosophical consequences of this are also noticeable, however. There are three problems with this:

1. Dispositional analysis of mental states
2. Perfect Actor scenarios
3. Armstrong's Problem

With Behaviorism causes become a little tangled. For example: X is in pain = X is disposed towards behavior. Unfortunately (for the Behaviorist), behavior in this sense becomes looped around by demanding a further mental response. In other words, what the Behaviorist cannot avoid is the perpetual, causal, and cumulative association of our actions with our thoughts. They do not recognize the relativity between mental and physical states.

Another case of mental disposition is with the Perfect Actor. Here the person's mental state is 'observed' to be identical with their outward behavior. However, inside they are actually torn by grief, holding a Master Degree in stage performance, fooling everyone.

Armstrong kindly told us how inert this field is. By ignoring internal processes all we achieve is a static account of external manifestation. Crucial to any study of the mind should 'obviously' involve its workings.

In effect, Behaviorists are putting the stimulus or reward, food, as cause of the response of crying in a baby. Nowhere is there a mention of mental events.

Likewise wrought with confusion is Materialism. By isolating their investigation to mere neural processes, however fascinating, they cannot grasp the conscious processes of the Mind.

Neural processes are considered type identities. When equated with other general processes such as Consciousness the two together become a type/type identity. To say these two are the same is to say all the rest: If the general statement is true then it is possible to deduce the particular. In other words, this type/type identity position does not allow for token Physicalism. Token Physicalism acknowledges a multitude of separate physical entities such as brain processes. It does not say the particular token brain process is mental. What is true for the general must lead to the particular within the same theory is what deductionism and reductionism is saying. This is false.

In other words, if a general mental state does not follow the same laws as the particular mental state and vice versa then you have a basic violation. Mathematic's, like the standard equation, if $A = B$ and $A = C$ then $B = A$, can prove this, theoretically.

However, this reduction of the conscious processes solely to neural firing falls apart when examined closer.

Functionalism tries to be discreet. It offers to us a Universal Program given to us by Turing, The Turing Machine. Like Orson Well's 1984 it sure is efficient! By applying a supplied quantity of predicates and variables we can come up with any proposition. Closely associated in dryness to Verificationist Syntactical Algorithm's (as opposed to alpha rhythms) the true semantics of the whole thing is lost to 99.9% of the population. All we have to do is input State01 and S02's within Psychological Theory 'PT', wait for the ticking and clicking of the internal mechanism and wham bang thank you *man* we get the sum total of the parts is...

This excessively generalized withdrawal from any mention of our dear mind, feelings, emotions, thoughts, ideas is great in logistics. And sure, it describes Robotic's to the tee. Where is the emotion, though? This is meant literally. Within our Mind are two halves and multiple sectors; one cannot describe our Mind's only in terms of Logic. In fact, most people are emotionally driven. Where is the experiential? Mathematic's can never account for the magnitude of the individual experience of our emotions.

All of these accounts demonstrate the inadequacy of Reductionist Biological Psychiatry as a Methodology for human mental states by either ignoring the problem all together or over-complicating it; they never get at the actual cause of the trauma, the trigger event, the switch which suddenly goes off and makes Little Johnny do a fender bender. They only dump pills on top of layers of suppressed memories and bad experiences.

To give a few general arguments and alternatives to Reductionist Biological Psychiatry let us consider Mentalism, Phenomenalism, David Lewis's, Mad Pain, Martian Pain, and U.T. Place's, Is Consciousness a Brain Process?.

U.T. Place gives us a good point when he points out to us the usage of the word 'is'. This word can be used in the definitional, strict, sense or in the analogous, compositional, way. He acknowledges the existence of a reference to Mind in these three points (pg. 56 Beta):

1. You can describe your sensations and mental imagery without knowing anything about your brain processes.

2. Statements about one's Consciousness and brain processes are verified in entirely different ways.

3. There is nothing self-contradictory about the (false) statement: 'X has pain but there is nothing in his brain'.

In effect, you can say the Mind is like some *thing* without having to do away with it completely.

David Lewis's gives us on pg. 83 section VI four points about the classification of a Being within a System. His point is, for every Being in X Body, pain is experientially different. What he says is the proper way of going about the Mind Body Problem is generating a System, like his, to allow for different experiences. If the Martian has a hydraulic system, Human's a brain state or mental state, get it a Mental State, a Madman or Mad Man a non-typical cause and response, and a Robot Circuitry, such is fine, just don't eliminate! A true Science Of Behavior does not ignore the mental phenomena.

This leads us to Phenomenalism. Parallel to Nagel's, What is it Like to Be a Bat? (pg. 145 Beta), the nature of the Subjective Experience is crucially important. Paramount in this is the mental phenomena which includes all the Sense Data. It is also Universal. Individual Mind's do not have to be isolated from the realm of provable accepted Science; it is without question it is 'something' or 'like something' to be another Creature so it does exist. Since we know these 'private' states do exist we can then begin exploring them.

To counteract Reductionist Biological Psychiatry nonsense is, as well, Mentalism. We all have Intent, the will to do something, Free Will, in varying degrees. Ah, what a cute little Noobie… To obliterate the Mind, Emotion, Feeling's, Thought, Ideas is to also destroy Intentionalism.

It is absurd to deny Mentalism, Phenomenalism, Mental terms and/or references to the existence of Mental Reality's, see Dream World's too, for Reductionist Biological Psychiatry to try to leave this out of the Mind Body Subjective Objective Problem, is like trying to ignore Consciousness.

Consciousness and Self-Consciousness is the process of being aware of yourself and/or your environment to various degrees from Rock, Plant, Animal, Human to Alien. Reductionist Biological Psychiatry has barely touched on this.

Artist's And Doppelganger's

The dive into the black pit of shadow and darkness is an unfortunate plight of most humans; some exist perpetually in this twilight… The reason people fall into madness is because their ability to cope with, understand and control the world comes directly from their inability to cope with, understand and control themselves. In <u>Frankenstein</u> this is expressed in terms of the Scientist/Artist 'going beyond his grasp', the attempts of a mere ignorant mortal to conquer the secret of life and death. In <u>Dr. Jekyll & Mr. Hyde</u> this is portrayed as the Scientist/Artist as becoming the darker side of his dualistic nature.

There are several ways to show this with Frankenstein. Let us go through them.

One can look at it in terms of Jung, the shadow, and Freud, the triparted soul. Man is seen as a Monster. Frankenstein's monster is simply the externalization of his hidden libido, id. Its raw unchained chaos and wanton urges produces a primitive vile form apathetic to life. Ironically, though, Frankenstein must give release to this; it is like a foul addiction. On page 148, after being given an account of his creature's misery, he consents, despite all rational objection, to the creation of a female for it, 'I consent to your demand, on your solemn oath to quit Europe forever, and every other place in the neighborhood of man, as soon as I shall deliver into your hands a female who will accompany your exile'. There are more holes in that logic than a sponge. This essay could be filled with refutations of that sentence; one should suffice: Who is to guarantee the creature will keep its promise? Frankenstein is working on soul faith, the sign of succumbing to an alternative motive. It is definite he is a victim to his unbridled scientific experimentation. He is a slave to his addiction for he undergoes severe negativity, and in isolation away from all friends or family, to accomplish it, on page 164: 'In this manner I distributed my occupation when I first arrived; but, as I proceeded in my labor, it became every day more horrible and irksome to me.'

In loss of control of himself he loses control of his world.

The ever prevalence of our dualistic nature is another explanation. In spite of its omnipresence how many people are aware of the intricacies, say, have a comprehension of the system of all dualities? Frankenstein falls dramatically short of this understanding of himself; he cannot hope to succeed with his creation. Frankenstein is filled with dualism. A comparison, known as vertical dualism, can be drawn up as follows: Father-Son, Scientist-Invention, Artist-Artifice, and Frankentein-Monster. This relation and the lack of understanding by Frankenstein is in the following on page 53: 'I doubted at first whether I should attempt the creation of a being like myself, or one of simpler organization; but my imagination was too much exalted by my first success to permit me to doubt to give life to an animal as complex and wonderful as man.' 'Blinded by Science' and 'delusions of grandeur' spring to mind. Frankenstein is not even considering the consequences of such a thing. In this his reason fails.

Frankenstein shows in subtler fashion another cause of our madness which comes from an inability to cope with, understand and control ourselves. This is the terrible affliction wracking this culture. It is the lack of a Mother and/or Father. So the reader does not immediately scoff, let us present the quotes first on page 100: 'Remember, that I am thy creature…' And, to quote a particular poetic presentation by Professor E. Newton, 'Without Father finds himself alone in a terrible world without any security… In effect a monster… No model how to live, no family, no explanation for existence. Where are my friends? What am I?' That about sums up the resultant madness of a complete lack of parental coping, understanding and control.

How could Frankenstein's beast be any more than a monster?

Dr. Jekyll & Mr. Hyde, a similar basket case, approaches the same problem via the inner pathways.

In the classical sense, we have the dualistic mirror image of human. Here, the character walks down the dungeon corridor 'her' face twisting in suppressed pain as psycho-manic urges pulls 'him' onward to futilely face his nemesis. Eritos and Sanitos battle on in the human psyche, one pulling up and the other down. The Gordion knot of Philosophy clenches your pounding heart. You 'fall' as a pit opens beneath your feet. This book is the archetype of this Cartesian, Descartian dualism. The world is the demonstration. In Prospect, The Tempest, 'This thing of darkness, I acknowledge as mine.' Since dualism is just a fact of life (and death), the 'doppel' nature of our existence becomes the cause of our madness. You cannot rationally control the irrational self: They are opposites. On page 44, paragraph one, Jekyll relates, 'The most racking pangs succeeded: a grinding in the bones, deadly nausea, a horror in the spirit that cannot be exceeded at the hour of birth or death… I knew myself, at the first breath of this new life, to be more wicked, tenfold more wicked, sold a slave to my original evil…' Apparently what is occurring is fairly adverse to the spirit. And before this on page 43, last paragraph, is the statement describing the nature of this, 'Enough then… of lower elements in my soul'. When Dr. Jekyll drinks his potion he releases these forces. Trouble is, because of the potency of his darker self he is pulled too far in.

He cannot control the strength of his opposite self and plunges into the vortex.

Again, we can resort to Freud and Jung. Freud tells me I want to return to the womb whence I came, the ultimate satisfaction of his libido drives. The Id wants, the Super Ego does not. We are released due to the intervention of a useful commodity called Reality, the Ego. Unfortunately, the price is being in a continual state of 'Grrrrr' in the Middle World's. Jung describes to us the Persona and Shadow. In this story, the house of Jekyll represents this. Dr. Jekyll's back entrance is the dilapidated building Mr. Hyde uses to enter his laboratory (pg. 25). Dr. Jekyll's house can be seen as a fine Victorian facade with a dump for his backyard. Too bad Dr. Jekyll has not the perspective of these two Psychologist's; he is the rat. In fact, Dr. Jekyll is far too obsessed (and addicted) to have much concern for any philosophical or psychological comments on his condition on page 46: 'The pleasures which I made haste to seek in my disguise…' This is indicative of Dr. Jekyll's total subjection to Mr. Hyde. The result of all of this is the complete loss of understanding by Dr. Jekyll. What objectivity, possible recompose, could benefit him is lost. Once again madness reigns.

The diabolic structure of Dr. Jekyll & Mr. Hyde is the sheer epitome of lack of coping, loss of control and understanding of oneself. To quote Professor E. Newton again, this statement gives a good description of the balance between self and the world in terms of lack of coping, loss of understanding and control: 'If you live in the sepulchered city and don't let the jungle reverberate around you, you will be worn down.' There are two forces going on in this story. Dr. Jekyll completely loses it (pg. 54) because of the inevitable insanity, and possibly worse, which comes from the battle in his psyche.

Both stories have dominantly dualistic themes. This is fine for it is an accurate picture of how human sees life. Human will 'overreach' and 'succumb'. Unfortunately, as Frankenstein and Dr. Jekyll & Mr. Hyde show us the cost of tampering with Nature, is loss of self.

Human Sanity

We are products of Nature.
In every way.
To go against that is destructive to us.
What is Nature?
Nature is what occurs, naturally.
Earth, Water, Air, Fire and Ether.
To go against this is destructive to us.
Wow, I could not guess.
But what I am really starting to question,
Is the Sanity of Humanity…

With Modern Society, with Human's (un)succesful battle versus Nature, we have isolated ourselves from the bad, evil and dangerous Elemental Forces of Nature.

In a building there is no direct Sunlight, there is no fresh Air, it is recycled, there is no Earth with its multitudinous plants, there is no clean, natural and fresh Water. Even the ether medium is now funneled through our hyper modern devices.

Due to the previous primitive nature of Humanity we constantly feared and fought the Element's of Nature when they are in fact our best friends; now we only try to control them but then in the worst possible non-sustainable renewable ways. We keep on filtering and filtering while still polluting but never really 'clean' their source up… One of the worst examples, as far as I am concerned, in the beginning of the 21st Century is the Gulf region in America.

To show how the Element's of Nature, thus obviously including all other Element's if used the right way, are our friends I will use a number of examples and arguments.

Where is one of the most favorite places for human? The Beach. Florida are some of the most common and popular holiday resorts, not to mention the countless other paradisiacal beaches and hot places. At a beach all 5 most common Element's are present at their most.

We are also very much attracted to Nature vacations, Sport vacations and anywhere where we can get outside underneath the sky and stars to refresh our bodies and minds. It is revitalizing, this is why many say that earlier generations were of a stronger stock, though nonsensical since their lifespans were on average much shorter. Many also now suffer from a great quantity and quality of modern sicknesses and diseases from the 9-5 Society where we are inside and sitting all the time. The combination of all this artificial reality, isolated, protected and excluded from the Element's of Nature, or naturally occurring Element's, in combination with poor diets, stress, too much science and technology, entertainment and digital digital digital devices unending leads to question the problem with Human Sanity these days…

Could it be we are quite dangerously isolating ourselves too much from Nature, not to mention wrecking, polluting and destroying our vital life sources in it? The next worse example at this time is the Amazon…

For a Human to remain sane, exposure to the foundations of our Life is necessary on a daily continual basis.

To strive, struggle and stress all year, for some 12+ hours per day just for money money money, just so as to have 2 weeks of Beach Time is not sufficient. If those two weeks of intense elemental exposure did not occur then people would be in a very bad state indeed.

And some do not get the opportunity because it is too expensive. Such is degenerating each and every day our Human Sanity. Such leads to increased fights, battles, conflicts and wars. Such leads to a dysfunctional Economy.

Why is Humanity subject to such Slavery? It is/was only 10 times worse with the African Americans and other previous colonies. Now we slave away 8-12 hours per days for a measly low average middle income and are expected to pay for auto, wife, children and all the other needs and wants, like a flat panel (total system for some quality in 2011: 32" Flat Panel + BluRay Player + 7.1 Surround System = €2500,00 at a min of). What is one supposed to do, only read a book from the library?

Around us to augment the problem is corruption, inflation and failing Governement's and economies plus terrorism. It strangely reminds one of WWI and WWII except that now, the greatest of ironies, Germany is practically the strongest Country in the world…

What is of the utmost importance for Human Sanity is the increase in the sustainability and renewability and exposure to the Element's of Nature in all City's: Try just walking down a (non-) busy street these days, there has never been more traffic… Office buildings with insufficient fresh air should be renovated or demolished. More grass and tree plots with real actual Earth should be planted everywhere; you can even stick parks and solar panels on roofs. Trees are the best plants, next to phytoplankton, to assist in Planet Earth awareness and increase Human Sanity to prevent this mass suicide. And not Trees coming out of cement, or even worse that so-called 'genius' plan to grow fake plastic Tree Farm's which generate oxygen. A Tree does not enjoy growing out of cement, would you?

Or, is there now only cement brick stone steel and glass on all sides of the street you walk down? One Central Park is just insufficient with all the Fossil Fuel's.

Another solution is decentralization. Throughout the History of Humanity this centralization even in the Middle Ages has caused massive Human sickness and disease and lack of Human Sanity. We could work in and near the city and live outside in more natural areas transported by an EM Propulsion Train. Very fast and very clean.

Put plants, trees and even flowers everywhere, they maintain themselves. It would be great and the average eyesore in each and every Modern Western Civilization City would also reduce palpitating cataracts and decreased Unhappiness.

Paint the buildings. This is cheap so everything is not god-ugly, dirty and grey, brown and black. The daily effects on the Human subconscious and mentality alone in modern society is not to be underestimated.

How about ponds? Fountains were abundant in previous cultures. Think of it as a 3D build game. How expensive is it, and how much does the lack of such things cost society, to have self-contained bubbling water troughs, ponds, fountains, where the water is continually circulating around? Simply do not turn it on on days which are too hot causing too much evaporation.

Do this everywhere. On a per per Community budget it is probably dirt cheap too with some Community volunteer and cheap labor jobs.

Do not stop creating clean, renewable and sustainable sources of Energy.

Unfortunately, the Oil Companies and their vested interests built up to date signed on irreversible and irrevocable contracts for 50 years into the future and are still controlling everyone and everything since the Industrial Age. Why do they not, like some are doing just now in 2010 and 2011, invest in and get the profit from Alternate Energy sources themselves? With the massive Industry caused it will make no difference who works for who. Many now do not care who gets the profits witnessing the daily destruction of Planet Earth, our only place to live for GOD knows how many hundreds of years still into the future, so long as better forms of Energy are introduced, utilized and maintained. Or do they?

Is this not the standard downfall in Human Sanity when their Greed takes over and everyone starts fighting for ownership. End Result: We are all dead in less than a century. Presently in 2014, 1 out of 8 cars are Hybrid's which is a staggering growth so there are little excuses to not develop in this direction. How long would it theoretically take to step over ALL automobiles? This is mind numbing and comes out bad considering how many vehicles there are in America alone.

How about the Sun? There is always something blocking it. Try finding a sunny bench just to sit on most days. Building should have a lot more glass, especially nice silver blue reflective glass. If your house also had a transparent 'glass' roof made of poly-compounds so hail cannot damage it such would be ideal! You could sit each day with the beautiful sky coming in. If it is rainy or stormy then you could roll a metal shielding over it and/or darken it.

All of these things are easily realizable in the 21st Century and many already last century but the blocked close-minded degenerating mentality of Human Sanity these days finds another way to prevent our development into the future. Maybe it is in our Nature to suffer excessively… Or, even worse, some form of bad evil hate to purposely cause such to others and then deny any possible alternate solution… Maybe, it just really is the inherent Greed in Capitalism which allows such blatantly.

We hear this bullshit everyday: There is no money for it.

Nonsense. In fact, in 2011, the Dutch Government while claiming budget cuts put another €200,000,000.00 into Military Development. You can even download their whole Defence document and read such in an article on Internet. But then, strangely enough, if you are older than 32 years old, despite all your experience, you are not allowed to join…

And such a figure is nothing compared to the rest of the Modern Western Civilization who since the beginning of the 21st Century, while pushing it in all foreign countries, conducted one non-democratic staged Election after another.

The statistics in the Netherlands, supposedly a Top 09 European Country according to even Obama, had a difference of only 8000 votes. They also refused to recount and/or acknowledge the defect erroneous voting machines which are extensively explained in a Scientific American article recently.

They then blame the immigrants who they let in, in the first place claiming they cost €480,000,000.00 due to a miscalculation by officials in the 70's who call it cheap unskilled labor.

Oops, there is no 'cheap', 'unskilled' labor left in the 21ˢᵗ Century, unless you are in Prison; still though a lot of such labor require first training.

I am sure, since I lived in The Hague for 15 years, that you can find similar statistics and processes and events in every Modern Western Civilization Country since 2001 when truly the world ended as we knew it with the barely recognized Millenium Prophecy.

Now, all Politician's and Economist's, say it is only going to get worse…

Who is fooling who? Yah, you mean for the low and middle man…

You mean, they want the money for their gold chests and the rest can starve.

Our so-called fight for equality in Democracy has never improved; the rich keep getting richer and the poor just sit and spin.

Not that I would want to sit and spin on most European Country's TV Channel's… Most just still have cable and it is all such 10-20 year old repeats on low resolution TV's for the vast majority of the populace who cannot afford the new devices. Only until very recently does Netherlands have digital TV with 157 Channels. Check the price tag in Euro's though for the whole system: 32" Flat Panel + Digital Receiver + DVD Player + 5.1 Surround System = €1000,00 at a min of) and that is not including the monthly subscription for various devices. Just so I do not have to go Insane and stare at a blank white wall I need to fork these figures out over these crap incomes after these stupefying tax levels AND THAT DOES NOT INCLUDE THE COST OF THE DVD'S AND BLU-RAYS! These go for €9,95 - €29,95 per fucking disk!!

Outrageous. And some dare say we are so Hyper Modern and at Near-Enlightenment. It is more like all the same lack of Human Sanity with different forms: Rich boys with rich toys and all their weapons is the sum total.

Then, to top it off, the people get the blame for buying all the cars which they are forced to just to get a job therefore Catch 22, they have all the power, energy, guns AND numbers and we get to slave away. Now, with Free Labor Job's to keep your Welfare, we are not even paid. If you went up to someone in Canada to date and said you have to work part-time or full-time with no pay they would definitely consider you cuckoo.

Still, the people are not entirely without guilt. My previous statement in a previous essay about 2.7 auto's per Family in America is not incorrect. That is just silly, going around the corner to the 24/7 convenience store in your car when you can walk or bike it.

The Consumer is powerful today. You, the Consumer's, have to demand these things not only for the Environment, but for the survival of the Human Species, and most of all your Degree Of Human Sanity. Not just in a month, but each day.

Consumer's have to also be better educated, not just by *only* 1 kilo of red meat per day.

Is it, after all, the quality or quantity of your time in this short life?

I for one do not need or want to sit in a white padded room with a custom-made white straight jacket doing nothing but blubbering and watching repeats of some WWII documentary in black and white at 40 HZ…

However, we also have no balance in our hyper accelerating development to the future and Space Travel.

Try not to Null Bomb Planet Exploder our only home in the mean time, though…

All of these things, such as recycling, can be done on each level in Modern Society. Just horrific, how many of you and businesses do not even bother to recycle still? I am still looking for FSC paper in each and every store, but no, €2,99 for 500 precious virgin white A4's plus ink plus glossy paper is the going rate for the chopping down of the lungs of Planet Earth.

Is, in fact, Human Insane? Are we not the only ones, on top of the food chain, who consume, devour, destroy, exterminate and annihilate all other things in its environment? Do we not wipe out and/or incapacitate all the weak and useless. Are we not just some cannibal? Do we not attack, flatten, dominate and take over all other races. I could reference countless historical Battles and War's on this one.

So much for the Sanity of Humanity cause now we are doing it with Science, Technology and Weapons much more powerful and energetic than just the Nuclear Bomb. See Science Fiction Film's and Series on various Energy Weapon's.

And how much does that War cost each day, again? We thought we already won in WWII... but as only recently revealed in International Medias and Internet such carries on in many Country's to date... The same left, middle and right keep killing each other rather than getting around a Knight's Round Table and discuss it.

Who is in charge of this Human Sanity? The title is better of being Human Insanity with very few exceptions like a sudden medical breakthrough. Except that they then have to pay more and more and more for their treatments, pills, delivery and care.

Well, everything and everyone rises (or falls) to their 'own level of incompetency'. Or, how many Weak Link's can you throw in an XP Homey Boy Outdate system before the whole thing just collapses... Many systems have still not updated and the Hacker has all the advantages with all the latest versions of cracked softwares.

Now, it is East vs West Stock Market's going back and forth the whole time with Multinational Corporation's suing each other for 'control regions'. Just like those Horror Science Fiction Movies predicted... They must have known ahead of time...

So, yes, things in the beginning of 21st Century suck on many sides, especially Nature, but if we simply APPLIED some of these solutions, without hearing unending bullshit of no Money for practicably guaranteed growth investment plans, then we could give Humanity a fighting chance to make a better future.

After all, was the past not even much worse where everyone sat around without anything doing what again but wait for the next War?

APPLY these and many other steps to Human Sanity.

Even better, do it not just for *only* Human Preservation. Sounds like an Indian Reserve.

Here is another underlying cause of the degeneration of Nature and thus Humanity along with it: Thus far Humanity has fought Nature for Survival. Since the beginning of dawn, Nature has posed a threat to our lives. Picture simply 500 B.C.E - 2000 C.E. with all the fetid, squalid, wretched, poor, starving, diseased and war stricken conditions.

Our fight, battle and war versus Nature has been successful...

We control the Element's Of Nature, now, not vice versa,

We no long burn, freeze, hunger and starve in the plains,

We are Lord's of the World, not a single Species can challenge our position,
Our dominion over all lesser creatures has not failed,
There is Nothing more powerful than us,
Now we can turn our eyes to the stars and the Alien's…

BUZZ! ERROR! Thanks for playing!

And, P.S., thanks for all the FREE Entertainment! This phrase is inspired by you know who. Nature is infinitely, if not just near-infinite, more powerful than us. Without it, we are Nothing. That is because we are in it. Nature is the only thing there is, it is Everything. You cannot get away from it, except die and free your Spirit and/or Soul but then do you not still just come back! Many Religion's and Philosophy's support this.

Any attempt to escape from Nature ensues in Death. In the case of Stupid Humanity in its Sanity Of Humanity a pathetic act of Self-Genocide.

Look at all of the Symptom's… Yet, still, no one solves the Causes. And band aids ain't going to help.

What are you going to do, put it back together with glue and tape?

Goodbye Planet Earth, goodbye Humanity.

Well, primarily unwell is the Human Sanity, Nature CAN be our ally, even our best ally.

Nature also being a Stupid Beast, it certainly is not going to say 'No'. Simple Cause and Effect, one of the most ancient Law's Of Nature which we still barely control is the key. There are no Politic's in Science, Mathematic's, Physic's, Biology, Chemistry, Astro-Physic's and/or any other field which is not ruled by the petty whim of stupid greedy Humanity. We should have unilateral development for the sake of the future of Humanity, not just short-term gains, or there will be no future for our children.

Now is the time, or suffer our own Extinction, where we can learn to work WITH Nature. We can only hope to channel or funnel all its Power and Energy, not fully *control* it like a bunch of Power Freak's.

Control and Dominance is one of the greatest illusions and delusions of the Sanity of Humanity.

Now we can, with more Knowledge and not Power, the huge error in that expression, learn to supply everything we need and want for Humanity all the way into the Solar System. Knowledge does not per se lead to Power to Corruption to Armageddon.

Knowledge also leads to a much better understanding of the Universe so we, now just a child of the stars, can grow into the next Galaxy's without destroying it or much worse, oh what a great tragedy is Humanity, ourselves…

Money-Freedom

Let us have a World which has no Money…

At first reaction, it sounds like ludicrously, secondly absurdity and finally impossibility.

I can also crack jokes, that is why I defined The Free Show.

But, technically, do not forget, the future has ONLY Credit's.

Now you pause, wait a second, how is that possible? Is he once again using damn fine argumentation to convince of the most far out in left field hypothesis like some continuously drunk Crazy Canuck?

No, really, the whole system is already going towards 100% Credit's. There is already no more actual gold, silver, gems and/or resources to back up the Currency. One of the more funny things I heard from a Family Member was that some English Diplomat actually sold ALL of the Gold Reserves at a very poor price down the river to some other country only a decade or so ago…

All Food, Shelter, Clothing, Medicine is Free.

All Education is Free.

All Entertainment is Free.

All Free.

Once again, at first it sounds completely ridiculous: Ceaser's Wraith would turn around in his grave and go on a rampage.

Yet, how many of these are already FREE on Internet?

Now you pause again, going wait a second, are we on a crash course with total disaster or is this why practically every Economy on Planet Earth is horrifically failing. It is so bad some now seriously take the breaking up of Europe inevitable and any EU Country can now be tossed out. I can hardly imagine a State in America being tossed out or asking once again for Independence. See the Greek affair and others might follow.

Yes, it can be done, in this Day & Age. It would simply mean, if you are able, you do some suitable Career for a scaled Credit amount in a 100% Credit System. Just to take a figure, let us say a Solar Panel Technical Engineer gets 100,000 Credits per Year. I am not saying that should be the amount for an entirely new well-balanced Credit System would have to be defined. If it was done right then maybe it would not suffer from all the pitfalls of the Bust/Boom Stock Market's.

Stock Market's as you have read recently also play with completely fake virtual non-existing Money and Credit's.

The problem is they are spending it before it exists. See Real Estate Scandal's and Crashes.

Money was introduced by Ceaser. Why? Him being one of the most famous Dictator's and World Conqueror's, others love him for 'Citizenship', he did to install Central Authority and to abolish Bartering. Well, he succeeded at neither due to the continual Spirit in people for Freedom and Liberation. It still takes two to make a thing go right, you can still just give a gift and the last we checked Central Authority is so tied up with more sub-paragraphs, holes, loops and exceptions that no wonder Anarchist's are practically deciding the fate of the world; one more wrench thrown in and 'Kaboom' there it all falls down with another Domino Effect.

Where do you think the expression 'Fist of Power' comes from? Not just Communism or Corporate America, since the fist is holding a bunch of crunched dollar bills, that fist is holding a wad of 1000's. It is a statement of their vastly superior Power and Wealth with the total Injustice and lack of People Right's, Freedom's and Liberosity's. And P.S., Fuck Peace cause that War Machine will never end. In fact, the Mechanized Military will develop into the Laser Military in the future and bring our Human Warfare to Space.

However, it will be as most Expert's and Intellectual's predict be driven by Credit's, not Money. You will have plastic cards, chips and a bank account only.

Arguing Credit's as a type of Money is semantics, it does not change the fact that the system will be nowhere the same with literally NO Cash. It will be all Real Identity's, Virtual Identity's and Card's with digital bank accounts.

So, watch out for that Eye In The Sky, alright…

We also have a joke going here in The Hague that due to the rising costs of the health care system, and the total irresponsibility of most heart patients, that there will be in the near future a Supermarket Card. If you buy red meat as a heart patient therefore a beep will go off and the cashier will say, 'Sorry Sir, but you are not allowed to buy that product!' One can picture all the beeps going off continuously.

Money makes a System a Central Authority where the lives of everyone can be regulated by an elect few who determine its distribution through various measures such as Interest Rates, Dollar Values and Salary Level's. With Inflation the board is nicely tilted so as to guarantee the end results.

Logic and Reason are not always the guiding factor.

As observed by many most decisions are in fact decided by Emotion.

Such is the nature of Central Authority. They argue we cannot function without it. Our response is: Since which century? Nowadays, with the advent of Information Technology there is no need (and little want) for such primarily central functioning.

If we want to have a completely Free System, a completely Free State Of Existence, no pun intended, then Money has to go. And it will, maybe not in this decade but most Expert's and Intellectual's predict even by the middle of the 21st Century. The only thing still slowing everything down is all that red-tape.

And it is not only us who want it: Your Government right now is seriously discussing and debating the major problem of Tax-Free Black Money and the Black Market. If you had any idea how much Money is circulated through all of such, i.e. Drug Tourism, then you would fall off your chair backwards and near-instantaneously go white stiff and rigor mortis.

No one can be put in jeopardy again by the one who is paying the axe man.

On the other hand, it sounds like possibly the worst Prophecy also coming up in the near future: New World Order.

Still though, is it not inevitable? Would you prefer Anarchy? The Middle Ages? The Renaissance? While having their Golden Age the pyro-technics in the background was most spectacular.

Or another good joke I still like: I am just here for the Spectacle. How much did we pay??

It should not be possible to govern People's lives with the Absolute Authority of Money. This allows one individual to have extreme Power over many others.

Who can trust one Individual? That is worse than Fascism and Communism put together.

Here is a proposition for the Free System: The only requirement, for those able, for each Citizen of a Country is to work a certain number of hours per week for a certain quantity of Credit's contributing to some part of the Free System. This is decided by the Citizen's Genetic's, Talent's, Skill's, Education, Work Experience, Need's and Want's which is determined through Relative IQ Test's. A Relative IQ Level, there is rarely ever an Obective IQ Level, is how able you are in your field of choice.

All the parts can be reduced to Need's and Want's.

The number of hours of your work and Type Of Work gives that Citizen the Privilege of going to any store and buying anything in any quality and quantity at a max of that Citizen's expendable Credit's. Non-expendable Credit's are needed for your Need's, like Home and Food. This can potentially solve all Homelessness since you can't touch those amounts, otherwise people will be tempted by everything on Internet.

As we see now in the over-production and incredible abundance of i.e. Food in the Modern Western Civilization, you are being very badly ripped off on a daily basis, what will simply occur if you picture all the shelves emptying is they will simply fill up again with increased production; there is no reason this will stop with correct methods applied for even another hundred years. Unfortunately though, razing, stripping and pesticides still have the upper hand which is badly wasting and poisoning our Environment.

Remember that Nobel Prize Winner for the breakthrough in Grain Production. He, too, thought it would solve World Hunger. But, of course, Politic's prevents simply a pipe being built with an Auto-Train which delivers excessive, after date and/or not needed and/or wanted food products to developing countries. There is recently only one breakthrough. For the first time Russia has built a pipe which is selling gas to Netherlands and other countries. They are also talking about a potentially very strong and powerful, not to be underestimated, Euro-Asian Economy. This is in no little thanks due to the co-ordinated efforts of Rutte, Minister President, and Putin, President, himself. Opposition, of course, gives out false allegations that he wants to make himself the next Tsar of Russia. Unfortunately, though Ukraine then happened and even NAVO Country's are being threatened as he chose to go with a War Machine instead.

Well, what is one supposed to do without Resources?

Also you think there will be a lack. Think again. Modern Western Civilization is synonymous with excess; Inflation Rates are kept artificially high to maintain prices and if not then they get all the eggs and toss them out on the street as forced by bosses. We pay here about €2,00 for only

12 eggs which is absurd considering about 10 years ago only with the Guilder instead of the Euro Inflation Zone. What will it be in the future?

For Citizen's, who are able, Work is mandatory.

Many of these points already indicate it will also not result in the completely unmotivated Communism and/or massive Welfare System.

This is also decided and determined by Relative Physical Test's. Objective Physical Test's also rarely exist unless we can find some prime genome which is hazardous water leading to more Racism and Discrimination.

With increased production more people will be employed. As the massive resurgences of getting free-bees, free loading and free shit fade, since Work is mandatory for those who are able, production and profits in Credit's will grow with the steady increase in population just as with any new successful product line. Balance will return and Job's will return providing more Human Need's, Want's and Desires rather than only Material Acquisition, such as Creativity and Culture and so on.

We are already seeing much evidence, if not proof, of this with Internet and the massive growth of Social Medias. To crack another joke, well at least it is now the end of spamming cause apparently, due to Common Interest's, I can now type in Relevant Keyword's and plug all of my own shit unending simply based on the color 'black'. Competition will be better balanced, one based on quality and quantity of product, not just money driven like American Election's.

This 'Free System', 'Credit System' meaning something else and being an undesirable title due to the post-capitalistic fall out system, is probably the best title for it. It has a sort of Positivism in it, rather than all the unending pessimistic Negativism pulling the system down by first premise already i.e. population growth leads to the end of the World: Well, no, population growth leads to the colonization of Space.

Thank you very much, end debate: By Natural Selection the required Geniuses and Specialist's to pull off the Elite Colony Spaceship requires more like 70 billion population.

This Free System will effectively eliminate Unemployment, eliminate Central Authority, eliminate the vast majority of Crime (What is there to steal? It is Free!) and bring Society to an advanced development of Nature, Culture, Human Potential, Material Wealth and other Non-Material pleasures which are necessary for Humanity and are severely lacking across the board in this Money-Based System.

The System's of Green Money, Bartering, Credit (Spend Money before you got it) are essentially the same as the stacking Coin-Based System as they all follow the same premise of using some exceedingly imbalanced and highly relative Abstract Value to determine the value of some product based on Bust/Boom and Supply/Demand.

This is no longer applicable in the 21st Century of the Modern Western Civilization: We now have, quite literally, an unlimited supply of each and every last product in each and every last store in each and every last Country. Look around you for all the proof you need and tell me if you want to go back to even the 20th Century or before?

Thus, it is only logical that, like Lincoln and Jefferson, we need a new defined System for new times. And, no wonder if you base your laws on that century with Locke and others like Smith that your System's are failing.

With this system which should be called the Free System, though Free Democracy (see previous essay in 1st Part of Evolutionary Essays) also sounds good, the only thing you have to do, as described above, as a Citizen, who is able, is to Work 20-40 hours for Credit's in a suitable field. I, myself, am stuck on Welfare due to Sickness And Disease which in Netherland's is presently bearable but when you look at other Country's it is severely lacking and you might as well go to the Food Bank just like the Middle East.

For those who want to earn more Credit's, nothing is stopping you: The more you put in the pot, the more you get out.

You could probably pull it off with the Percentage System, only, but fair enough, it obviously requires development and would be quite a complicated system.

But please, don't make me slave and starve away… And, even worse, where are your Social Security's for all those NOT ABLE in those Country's?? How about let us just be a good blunt Canadian and such equals Mass Slaughter.

I am not a Social Democrat. See one of the first Evolutionary Essay's where I state that the word 'Social' has an irrevocable bad name due to WWII. I am not even Left. I am more like a Middle Free Democrat. The party is even decided: FPD or PFD standing for Freedom and Peace Democracy or Peace and Freedom Democracy depending what mood we are in. Nowadays, it is obviously primarily FPD, because they will never have Peace and we have to keep Fighting For Our Freedom on each level and each day.

And, if you want to crack jokes about Middle then so can I, how about you take the Absolute Middle concept and apply to each and every last sector. Is it not simply a question of whether your Contract is fulfilled or not? I mean, as long as I am not working for or paying that Enemy or Terrorist then just get the job done!

However, also in the 21st Century, the concepts of Left, Middle, Right have become antiquated yet new Politician's still keep trying to argue it when it is Economy which is the ruling factor and not your Politic's.

If you want to earn more Credit's then do the work. End Of Debate. QED. QER.

The Free System can be this simple, but just like Marx, and I am definitely not a Marxist, they will try to twist and abuse ever last word for their Power and Greed in the Human Sanity Complex as described in the previous essay.

Or even better like the famous Rougeaux, 'So much of Democracy is based on the good will of Humanity'. So true, and ironic, because there is none and then his dual acceptance of GOD in the last chapter to appease the Church granted him lenience.

Well, in the 21st Century, we do not have to appeal to their failing infrastructure anymore, nor yours in any other Religion, which is where I differ: Does your Religion put Food on my table, does your Religion give me Work, does your Religion grant me enough Need's and Want's so I maintain my Human Sanity? Does your Religion do anything for me except conduct more Holy War's since we and they are not abiding by your tenets written granite with no flexibility for daily application; how many Arab's drank beer, wine and alcohol and still do, not just externally apply it for Medicine? Am I supposed to only smoke cigarettes, pot and opium because that was stated in a far previous century?

If so, then we do not have a problem with your Religion.

Last we checked though, the only thing not Kösher about your meat are the Gold Coin's.

At least, though, we can apparently thank India and Islam for Welfare. Though did not the Chinese also invent that?

And, how is your Christianity going to recover from all those centuries?

Well, as a Canadian, I am not a Racist or into discriminating: Kill all the ugly demon faces of Racism and Discrimination for there is no such thing in the 21st Century as a Non-Multicultural Cosmopolitan Society.

What are you going to do say 'No' to Arabian Mathematic's which dominated the entire millennium from 0-1000 C.E. and is still determining Hyper Modern Quantum Mathematic's?

Free Democracy does not tolerate your Race and Species bias. Better said, is your Stupid Humanity simply trying to wipe them out. This is why we should also think in terms of Species. Dominance means Guardianship, again, yet we only devour all lesser Species, the same insatiable blood urge to suppress and repress lesser Human Races.

Money, you are wiping them out for Money. For what, some Manic-Depressive sense of Self-Preservation cause you have to acquire 13.5 billion dollars for a rainy day?

Money is the root of all Evil today is the Numero Best Understatement Of The Century.

The Free System, or Free Democracy (see previous essay in 1st Part of Evolutionary Essays), will contribute to the much needed De-Centralization, advancing Modern Society to a connection with Technology and Nature as more and more Community's, real and virtual, spring up again and again and everywhere with people getting all Types Of Work in a near-unlimited quantity and quality of Career's and also spending with the also mandatory Recreation Time, which should be at a min of 4 weeks per year for each and every Country, being outside, contemplating, solving and progressing Art, Culture, Technology, Nature and Human to make a truly Free and Peaceful World.

One can even tentatively state that technological and natural advancement would not be hindered by Research and Development Budget's. This is because each Country will then start developing and producing excesses beyond imagination, not just so-called Golden Ages in History which raped other Cultures to acquire such.

One can only hope that all those Peoples, who will NEVER be able to pay for all your products in the Money System, will also fall under the Great and Good Wing's of Free Democracy.

Let us also pray that it does not turn into their Evil Prophecy of some New World Order, which is no different than some Totalitarian Authoritarianism.

Thanks to my God's, my Goddesses and GOD always above always looking down.

Coupled Pair's

Introduction

What is most interesting to me about Coupled Pair Theory's, next to the obvious prevalent unavoidable Dualism, is it is applied on a Quantum Existential level to particles and people and their paths and lives. Like Husband and Wife, Mother and Son, Boyfriend and Girlfriend, Man and Woman their entire fates and destinies and Karma seem coupled to each other for years and decades if not a whole life.

This also has potential theories about the beginning of Creation where after the Big Bang many particles split, divided, coupled and multiplied. Genetic's now is seeing the key to this in Gene Therapy.

The following parts will describe other coupled pairs which do not per se work together but can also be opposites, yet are still bound and attracted to each other by necessity.

Part 01
Scientist/Philosopher

All Math is quantitative. It uses numbers. Numbers measure things. Measurement is for quantity. It is necessary and helpful thus when controlling Energy and constructing Matter; the only difference if you are a Mage you can do it by will alone. Making parts for machines demands precision which could not be had otherwise, especially for Robotic's.

Also, since all of Nature is physical and physical means it has dimensions, Math is useful for giving relative quantities, which can come in handy when desiring to know the exact orbit of all the Planet's or weight distributions for construction.

Quantitative values are also useful for determining distance. Distance from one point to another allows the construction of something to be perfectly determined through relation.

However, Math is useless for qualitative values. Quality is exactly what the significance and meaning of that thing is. It is a relative quality.

Example: What is the substance Energy? Math could never answer that as it is incapable of determining the nature of a Substance, the relative quality. In fact, to date, despite all our hyper modernism no one still has any clue what Energy *really is*. The best attempt to date is a still unsolved Light Wave/Particle Theory.

Math could state what parts of that substance are and when and where which would give us clues as to what it is, however it could never explain what the Philosopher could answer: 'What is Life?' Not that Philosopher's per se have the absolute answer or the full story on this one and many attempts have been made but it is still a relative qualitative question and has very little to do with any quantitative argument i.e. saying the entire personality and identity of someone is based only on Biological Science, Psychiatry and Psychology, thus no better than a Robot, is blatant erroneous idiocy. It does not come anywhere near describing Consciousness and how about the Spirit and Soul?

Math could also not answer what other Scientist's can such as the Chemist: 'What are all those cells?' Though, once again, not that anyone has enough answers to cure anything these days or increase the Human lifespan beyond 78 average in the best Country's.

Since I also like to make people laugh, not just cry, I plan to live to 125 years of age. It's never been done so far, not even by the greatest Chinese Sage claiming Immortality. Yet think about the life extension pills coming on the market in the near-future. They will probably be more addictive then heroin and cigarettes and alcohol combined. In fact, there was already someone in the news who says he takes 75+ pills per day to reach this same end.

In my case, it would thus ironically end up being exactly 2099…, smirk.

Math answers, 'Where? When?'

Words answer, 'What? Who? Why? How?'

Part 02
Symmetry/Asymmetry

The philosophical symbols in the World are the symmetrical alignment, and asymmetrical alignment of the Spheres, where the points are i.e. the centers of the Spheres. Symmetry is a powerful Relation Of Forces which provides for Balance, and Imbalance. Balance allows for the maximal flow of Energy through Nothing, as you can have a very open shape which stays together due to its Balance, like in Architecture.

From Balance comes complementary continuance.

The symmetrical alignments of points are the regular polygons.

Each of the regular polygons has their points located in the Circle. They are fractions of a Circle. And the Circle is a fraction of the Sphere.

A regular polygon is a representation of the underlying geometric relation of the Balance of Energy. The Philosophy's and Religion's choose symbols which are regular polygons because they are the symmetrical alignment of the Spheres: Power and Energy Symbol's. There are so many examples, choose one yourself and try to figure out what it really means… See the table below too.

The regular polygons and their associated Philosophy or Religion coincide with the claims of Numerology. Back then, Numerology had nothing to do with the popularized New Age, I am definitely not a New Ager, but the actual secret and sacred Power's and Energy's was in each and all things, people, knowledge, life, death and time.

Based on the usage of numbers with wisdom i.e. Delphi Oracle with the Planet's and Constellation's you can predict many things. If you have doubts blow your mind away with what happens with the Planet's and the 2012 Aztec Prophecy: They line up. If this then also happens at the same time as Full Moon then the incredible Power and Energy of the Electro-Magnetic Force will surely cause the fault line to rupture. Brazil and the Christos Redentus statue apparently first go and then California gets hit. This could result in a tsunami and much death and destruction. There will then either be not much left of California or a whole new large Island drifting away from the coastline! This, fortunately, did not happen but many other simultaneous events did happen. There are many other examples in History when Planet's aligned and great changes or catastrophes took place.

However, a lot of predictions and prophecies except practically Nostradamus had a mild delay since back then they were unaware of the Time Dilation Effect. So, despite the fact even Scientist's say this major Planet Alignment will happen in December 2012 it could also happen in January 2013. Look at the number. 13 = Unlucky. Look at the date of the Haiti Earthquake. Look at the date of many other disasters and great events in the History of Humanity. Not only Numerology but also the position of the Planet's and Constellation's decide events on Planet Earth. I don't even need to argue Full Moon's and Eclipses which bring on even more events.

This is not superstition since those areas and regions are earthquake prone due to multiple fault lines in the crust which can be hit by Electro-Magnetic Forces.

Based on the usage of numbers, back then Numerology was even synonymous with Mathematics and it was all a part of Philosophy, a tool for demonstrating differences, there is essentially at a max of 19-20 symbols and numbers (plus 0 for a total of 20 or 21 possibilities) with their associated meanings and usages by Philosophy's, Religion's, Science, Mathematic's, Architecture and if you really think about it, it is quite difficult for any field to avoid using them somewhere. Chemistry is full of symmetry and asymmetry of chemicals in geometrical points and patterns, quite literally a Microcosm.

It is 19-20 since it is still unclear as to whether it becomes over self-redundant and can no longer be reduced at 19 or 20. For is not 20 simply 2 x 10?

Here is a table to show the numbers and symbols with their associated values and meaning. This is not invented but as stated drawn from many Philosophy's, Religion's and Science.

Number	Symbol	Elemental Association	Philosophy, Religion, Science	Explanation
20	Icosagon ☽☾○ ▤	Moon	Many Pantheons and Cultures.	Next to the Full Moon, many New Year's are based on the cycles of the Moon.

19	Enneadecagon	This finishes off the cycle creating a step up to the whole new level. Fairly positive, creative and constructive.	System's using Numerology though not too recognized as meaningful in most.	The first combined number to equal 10. This is also possibly the last non-self redundant number. Everything above at or above 20 simply repeats basic meaning and significance with small variations i.e. 133 is an interesting one.
18	Octadecagon ✝ 666	A Power Number divisible by 6 three times and have Symmetry.	Occult, Satanism but also many Religion's, Philosophy's and Science	This is the only number divisible by 6 three times, 666 being the number of Satan. Next to such it is very strong symmetrically and equals 9.
17	Heptadecagon	Luckiness in Balance and Equivalence	Systems using Numerology.	Once again 7 is Good and Lucky but 1 + 7 = 8 results in Balance and Equivalence.
16	Hexadecagon	Fluctuation, Chance for Good or Bad.	Numerological systems.	Using the rules of Numerology 1 + 6 = 7 which is Good but the actual 6 which is Evil gives you the possibility.
15	Pentadecagon	Evil, Negativism	Occult, Satanism and other systems.	Many numbers also add up, this one results in 6.
14	Tetradecagon	Double Lucky, Two Fold	Following various numerological systems.	This is also a very positive number representing 2 x 7 or your performance or numbers are up.
13	Tridecagon	Unlucky, Misfortune	This one is practically universal.	Like the number 6 this one has a very negative connotation and represents all those unlucky events.
12	Dodecagon Â	Clock, Time, Full Cycle	Almost all cultures who have the 24 hour clock.	The repetitive cycles in the calendar and Nature as divided into the 12 hours per half day, 12 months per year and 60 minutes is divisible by 12.

11	Hendecagon ‖	Spiritual and Mystical number	Druidism and Monk's.	This number is associated with spiritual and mystical achievement and empowerment.
10	Decagram	Perfection, One with All, Everything and Nothing	Judaism, Islam and Science with decimal system	This is supposed to be the number of GOD and has replaced all other Math systems as the most commonly used system.
9	Nonagon Q	Heavenly number, Divine Wisdom, Uplifting	Theosophy, Grecian plus other Religion's and Philosophy's, the upward spiral.	Divine Wisdom being Truth of the God's and Goddesses. Originated back in Greece, 3rd Century B.C.E Though who is to say Babylon and East did not already give this number great Power and Energy.
8	Octagon ·✳❀∞	Balance, Symmetry, Eight Fold Path, Infinity	Buddhism, a number of Philosophy's also give the octagon significance.	8 steps, levels, stages and parts of your Human progress. The middle path between two squares in Material Plane Of Existence to Infinity.
7	Septagon	Heaven, Chakras, Luck	Theosophy, Mathematic's applied to Chance Probability Game Systems.	7 levels and stages of Human development. However, these are only the material ones, 8 and 9 go to higher spheres.
6	Heptagon Y¬ÜP	Double Trinity, 6 dimensions, downward Spiral, in Numerology also stands for Evil. Hexagon.	Judaism, various Philosophy's and other Religion's give this number supernatural value. Math sees Hexagon as very useful.	Note the 'evil' superstitions with this number, meaning going down.

5	Pentagon ØÀ«	Occult, Magic, Good or Evil depending on alignment, Human, the 5th Prime Element Ether	Paganism, Wicca and the Church have greatly associated Good or Evil with this symbol. Science simply perceives it as Ether, though there is Debate over Time being 4th or actually 12th one.	The belief Human is composed of sets of 5. Other systems which also led to the 7th system.
4	Square o†Ê	Symmetry, Material, 2D, Earth, Water, Air, Fire.	Science and Religion grant great strength to the square. Also many Cultures, especially the Celt's and our Architecture is dominated by the square and cube.	The belief in strict Order, right angles, precision and other logic and simplicity of construction.
3	Triangle råæ	Triangle, Higher Self, Mind/Body	Islam, Trilogy, Mathematic's, Architecture, Pythagoras plus many other believe in the Power and Energy of the perfect triangle and variations.	Once again, the reduction of universal laws to the system, the most well known being the Christian Trilogy.
2	Line [¡ I	Circle, Life/ Death, Self-Consciousness, Dualism, Good/ Evil	I Ching, Taoism, Duality, Religion's, Philosophy's, Science fields, Literature, Film	The reduction of all Power and Energy interactions in the Universe to two Forces of Yin/Yang, and so forth. Self-Consciousness is Energy feedback looping unto itself.
1	Point .	Sphere, Oneness, Truth, Order, Perfection, Consciousness, Universe, GOD	Many Religion's, Philosophy's and Mathematic's.	The unifying of all fields of study for Human Evolution. One with Nature. Perfection being Immortality, Omniscience and Omnipotence.

0	Zero or Null $0\|\infty$	Nothingness, Final Liberation	Buddhism and Hinduism plus others.	Nothing is the opposite of Everything. Nothing has no limits.

Note: Not all symbols of various beliefs and systems can be represented in table so if you feel left out then know you are somewhere not forgotten!

Note: As to whether unique symbols exist for 11 - 20 is highly debatable for it is most likely they simply use combinations of the first prime 10 numbers.

Internet is a great source for these things these days since in the past it was all perceived as 'secret and sacred' or 'hidden and forbidden'. You would be surprised what you can find qua the meaning and significance of all numbers up to 1000 and how these have portrayed themselves in actual events in History. The most obvious example was the prediction by Nostradamus of the 1666 C.E. huge City fire in London; there are countless other examples. One has to ask oneself if GOD, the God's and Goddesses do not play with numbers…

Part 03
Astrology/Astronomy

In Antiquity, primarily Classical Rome and Greece, Astrology was seen no different as Astronomy. All the Planet's HAVE associated God's and Goddesses. For some reason, I think primarily due to the watered down pop crap Astrology in newspapers, that it is no longer officially recognized! Who is sacrilegious now? Like anyone can deny the effects and associations of Luna herself… Also who is to say there is *not* a Spirit and Consciousness embodied in Mother Earth: Look how she fights back against the massive out-of-control parasitical infection spreading across her surface.

Saying 'not', such is impossible, is once again the inflated Human ego complexes who claim to be the only sentient beings in the Universe. Well, no, in fact Humanity is just too primitive to be able to detect any other sentient life. We even wipe out all lower Species on this Planet and have not even figured out to date one single Animal Language. The best performance to date is teaching an Ape a number of word recognitions but we still have no clue what any of them are saying in their highly complex Bird Language calling it 'instinct' and 'survival mechanisms'.

Astrology, suffice to say, was used seriously by every Culture in History, except our own so-called Modern Western Civilization. For examples, the Aztecian Architecture, the Egyptian Architecture, the Greek Mythology, Chinese Astrology, Babylon, Rome, even the Celts with Stonehenge for it lines up with Laya Point's and you name it, everyone up to the 20th Century.

Then why is it, Modern Civilization, the Civilization of Science, does not take it seriously?

It is because of a lack of understanding of Electro-Magnetism.

Well, in light of what has been described in previous pages and with this explanation, Astrology can be put in the place it deserves. That is, a serious and recommended study in this society, too.

When you are born, the celestial bodies, the Sun, Moon and Planet's plus the Constellation's are in a very specific relation to each other, a specific pattern.

Each of these has an orbit, a plane, except the Sun which is the center of the Solar System. Their planes intersect and cross over each other, so do their large EM Field's, at various points in Space, including a point on Planet Earth at that juncture in Time.

In fact, some Scientist's go as far as to say, and are proving it, that each and everything are only interacting EM Field's. We are primarily 'empty' with such keeping us together. Only the equally negative charged rapidly swirling electrons give the illusion of solidity.

Electro-Magnetism and the EM Field's are manifestations of the same force in Nature. So, even if you absurdly do not believe there are Higher Being's then this scientific explanation still argues you under the table.

The problem is the West has to associate everything quantitatively, as described above, so they get very squeamish with the unavoidable qualitative values. However, I will grant agreement in one thing and that is there has to be a more refined objective system rather than just the 12 Houses in your Horoscope with the other Elemental associations and more reliable studies, tests and experiments done to generate evidence and proof. As I brought up at a Science Forum, what is the full Astrological Chart of someone born on Mars?

We cannot arbitrarily state and/or predict things by the 'mad chants' of one 'Witch or Warlock' only. We need fully developed computer programs analyzing the entire sky. There are already some good programs since 2000 but before Astrology can be taken seriously again by most it has to start accurately analyzing people, things and events, not saying, 'Tomorrow in the afternoon at lunch you will meet the love of your life...' Hurl, groan, moan, please do not make me throw up over everything, again...

What is known about Electro-Magnetism is it affects and binds particles across Space. A Magnet demonstrates this. Pretty nifty, that such a simple very common example which we learn at High School practically holds the secrets of the entire Universe and the future of Humanity.

Now, you know we are composed of Matter. You also know Matter can be transformed into Energy. And you know Electro-Magnetism affects and binds Matter. So, at the point where you were born, the Sun and Moon and Planet's and Constellation's are in an exact Electro-Magnetic Relation with you. In other words, your entire 3D Matrix or 3D Form, Mind, Body, Spirit and Soul bound into its vessel, is generated at conception into the DNA. This code, or this 3D Polygon, of you are and will become with all your strong and weak qualities is the most important determining factor on your life. You can also argue further that this is how your Karma works: What you did in the last life decides where in Reality you are born into.

Since Astrology is often too generalized and does not have a full system of defined dualistic qualities it is often scoffed at. Also, most books on it give you lengthy vague descriptions about what you will most *likely* experience or what qualities you *probably* have. Rather, give me a book with all of the qualities of an Aries at Full Moon (I suffer from this since my Aries in the Moon) then I will not get into trouble so much... But o.k., it still does (not) make me 'evil' or 'crazy' or 'dangerous' or 'out-of-control' or 'stubborn' or just 'PISSED OFF'. You should not judge me so harshly for such are Aries-like emotions only... Unless, of course, you combine Drug's & Alcohol into the mixture...

Thus, another way to put it which does not sound as corny as 'EM Relation' is, since you are Matter, your exact Electro-Magnetic Pattern is formed when you are born with its potential growth towards good and/or evil, weak and/or strong, water and/or air, poor and/or rich, Artist and/or Scientist. In other words, your Being's Construction, which is Physical and in many ways Virtual, is also according to most Scientist's now, determined by your Genetic's. For the rest of your life you are governed by your Electro-Magnetic Construction, your Electro-Magnetic Pattern.

Whereas environment and conditioning will always play a role in your opportunity and success it still does not take away from the argument of what your talents and skills and interests and performances are in... Your brain also is made up of such.

Your Sun Sign which has the strongest Electro-Magnetic Force, and take a look at the relative size of it in the Solar System, influences plenty of your life too. Your Ascendant, the rising sign at the eastern horizon, also is in some cases just as dominating and influential as your born sign and apparently it begins to take control at a senior age.

The Moon is closest but much smaller and it exerts the second strongest 'pull and push' on you. This becomes your 'Moon Sign'. Statistically proven, even crime rates go up at Full Moon plus many other calamities and even disasters. Still funny to me though as coined by a previous colleague of mine, 'Don't you know, you suffer from Full Moon Sickness.' Who does not such as periods... Well, men suffer it in their brains...

These two have the strongest influence over you often completely dominating and obliterating your Birth Sign. Your Birth Sign is where all the Sun's, the Moon's, the Planet's and the Constellation's Gravitational Field's intersect on the Zodiac Map.

Wow, what a coincidence. And, no wonder there is more to the picture than meets the eye. How are we supposed to define a fully comprehensive modern system when practically every day another heavenly body is discovered? Back then there were, remember, only 7 Planet's even!

Astrology should be given the chance to develop.

You can thereby also see it as your Electro-Magnetic Balance, that which all our other Magnetic Influences revolve around and that which compose our entire Being. Your Electro-Magnetic Pattern, of which your Birth Sign is only 1 factor out of many, is the also the only one Pop Astrologer's use in newspapers, therefore nonsensical idiot gibberish.

What you need to draw up your whole Astrological Chart is your exact date and time and location of birth! Who has ever bothered to do this?? Try it some day, you will be surprised how many things line up in your characteristics.

The Big Question, of course, is at what point in future Time do you measure for? That is a complicated problem and needs to be studied.

Yet, it could have far reaching consequences. If we, like the Delphi Oracle, could predict the so-called 'Blessing of the God's on the crops due to necessary sacrifices' then we could have another much needed Early Warning System. Back then, people were primitive and uneducated, most did not even write or read, so they needed such symbology. But now, if we can restore Astrology = Qualitative Astronomy to a working reliable Science we could even make a lot of money in stocks...

That is just to appeal to your Greed, how about the next Presidential Election?

The times, stage, level, epoch, millennium and era of the Evolution of Humanity are also determined by the entire Astrological Configuration.

To repeat the argument, you cannot have *only* quantitative values.

I would opt for Conception, the point where the sperm inoculates the Egg, and bondage, where the exact configuration of the chromosomes is implanted. Then wait… and grow… and mature… and mutate… and develop… what all your potentialities are or are not realized.

However, as stated, this full comprehensive system actually does not exist. What happens if we discover a 10th, 11th or 12th Planet? Does Astrology then have to modify itself again? Well, what does not update and/or upgrade itself?

Astrology simply has a bad name and has not been given the chance to develop into a fully functional and accurate system.

Part 04
Magic/Will

I am not talking about the 'sense of magic in the air' or 'do you believe in magic' or 'that has a magical aura' or all of the other highly Dungeons & Dragons dependent Fantasy Literatures, 3D Games and Film's these days.

I am not talking about Magic as wielded by an Illusory Stage Artist.

I am not talking about Miracles, which do happen, but is the realm of Religion.

I am talking about Magic, the real stuff.

Magic is the controlling of Matter and Energy by Will alone.

I am not talking <u>about</u> it.

What I hope to depict and describe is exactly how to gain your rightful developed innate latent Human capabilities and how Magic is real and potential.

Null. Nulling. Null potentialus ad majorus.

Exaltus majorum!

Still fun, cause it sounds like a Harry Potter spell, but I am also not talking about Wand dependent Magic.

True Magic is by your Will Power alone.

Some think Magic is synonymous with Paranormal Ability's.

These include: Photographic Memory, Telepathy, Teleportation, Astral Projection, Levitation, Flying, Planar Travel, Time Travel, Telekinesis, Clairvoyance, Super Human Feats and many others described in not only Literature, Film's, 3D Games and Comic Strip's but in Eastern Religion's.

Two Prime Factor's are involved: Source and Control.

Null can be a source, but obviously that is for Null Mages.

The Elemental's, thus read not Element's, can be a source and that is for Elemental Mages.

The only difference between Control methods is how they are channeled. A Civilization who only knows how to channel such Power's and Energy's through Technological Devices is at the beginning of the 21st Century.

The Source is the Source Of Energy you draw from. This is greater Energy than what your own Mind and Body can generate, it comes from below, all around you and above, because working Magic is parallel to Metallurgy. Such a thing you cannot do with only your own strength. In many instances, you can function no more than a channel or medium. In other instances, you can direct or funnel such externally for you can be twisted or possessed by such.

You cannot just take any Source: There are different types of Mages. Many try and simply destroy themselves on the spot or eventually. Why is this?

Well, for starters, you also have many associated Element's and Elemental's in your Mind, Body, Spirit and bound Soul. Secondly, you probably have no formal training like a Shaman and after much research, study, experiments and development the vast majority have come to an unanimous conclusion (again?) that the primarily drug/hallucinogen based path most likely leads to very not unreal brain damage instead of actual insight and ability.

And still, not one can prove on camera with witnesses that he or she can lift a small object off of a table with will alone…

In addition to such, for the necessary Balance in the Forces, Nature will not permit those of evil and destructive intent to gain any lasting significant capability of Magic, or Sorcery in this case. Likewise, Nature will not permit those of evil and destructive intent to survive, they will be relatively quickly annihilated or banned. They will be sucked down to the nether spheres of Higher or Lower Planes Of Hell.

If you want to also use the argument of God's, Goddesses and/or GOD then forget it, only one needs to show up and the parading pompous Sorcerer is incinerated near-instantaneously on the spot.

Once again, would you rather there be only Chaos, with Wild Mages dominating?

Trying to use other peoples Psychic Energy, or drawing from the Spirit World, the Dead or Undead, will also get you rapidly killed and sent off to a local Hell.

Theoretically, the only safe Source Of Energy is the Energy which is freely occurring everywhere and is freely available to all.

This is Nature itself, not its denizens.

Nature is near-infinite, if not infinite, and does not notice.

Nature's denizens like to have and keep their Energy and are not interested in parting from it or having it forcibly sucked out of their skulls.

This leaves, therefore, the substance of Nature itself, such which does not possess Consciousness. Pure Energy, maybe… except what is truly 'pure'…

Oh wait, one more reminder to those darklings, I was not entirely correct in the statement above, if you draw from psychic consciousness you will first go insane, then get killed, then go to the Hell Planes for your God knows how long, and thankfully…

So, to just wreck the argument my God is not your God so I can conduct unending Warfare on your head: Is that not the Demon God and/or Demon Goddess you worship?

Sucking Energy from others i.e. Psychic Energy is being a Vampire of some type.

Such is not Magic. Such is some form of Dark Black Evil Negative Energy Sorcery. And Mages, Wizard's, Priest's and Sorcerer's have never agreed with each other. I, however, much prefer the logic, reason and rational argumentation which we High Wizard's provide instead of your unending Incantation bullshit.

Or, oh no wait a couple rounds now, since I cannot Cast shit to save my life and need to Summon a Butterfly, a really big Butterfly to save the twat Battle.

The most common naturally occurring substances are, once again, the Prime Element's: Earth, Water, Air, Fire and/or Ether. With these in infinite abundance, it is impossible to destroy a Prime Element, why would you ever fall for all their lies?

Not to say that if you do not drink too much Fire Water that you do not go off your rocker but the difference still remains in Good Intent or Evil Intent.

Good Will and/or Evil Will in all of its shades of gray still decides the day.

Nothing is Black or White.

The whole Universe is just different degrees of gray.

The whole gray spectrum...

The Prime Element's have an infinite quantity and quality of Energy. They last forever and are indestructible. You can never get rid of any one of them in any one space. In all spaces you will find at least one of these, and percentages of others though even minute, and in Class M World's, the five all exist to promote Life.

Not Death and Destruction.

This World is rampant with Death, and Death Complexes, and we do not tolerate your evil and destructive presence. We shall fight and Battle you until you exit even the Middle World's and return to your Hell Planes.

Death may be the most powerful and negative energetic God but do you not think it is how you lived your life *and* how you go?

Thus anyone interested, if not fixated, addicted and obsessed, with Death cannot and will...

You know the story.

You know the movie.

The very quality of their Energy and their effect of Energy stops the Evil Wielder when the Good Wielder opens up to their Energy.

You know all those stories...

You know all those movies...

Those twisted Evil Sorcerer's who suck on other people and/or on the Spirit's/Dead/Undead are twisted by the very fact they chose those two routes which are hand in hand. Soon, you begin to have no value for Humanity and start cracking jokes about how you now have only 1/16 Humanity. Yet, you are not Immortal, and nowhere near, you suffer the worst yourself from all the Illusion and/or Delusion, in a matter of decades you will also just die and be judged by Osiris, or by whatever name the God of Death goes by in your Culture.

Or, even better, you will be swallowed whole and ripped asunder by your very own Demon God and/or Demon Goddess. Is that not his and/or her values, rules and laws?

In most cases, they are doing it for Power, not Energy.

This is the whole key to the matter. All of those irresistible temptations of Money, Power and Lifestyle has very little to do with Energy.

What did you choose for, Good or Evil, Cure or Sickness, well how about Power or Energy? Power ≠ Energy.

What is the difference between a Politician and an Economist?

The pursuit of Magic is not Power. True Magic is the actual controlling of Energy by Will alone.

This is not so I become some Rich and Famous Freak Show.

Necessary to the actual ability of Magic is opening to and controlling the Sources of Energy. The Prime Element's: Earth, Water, Air, Fire and/or Ether.

Much neglected until the recent zero-point-field theory is also Null. As described in my other Evolutionary Essay's think of it more in terms of Potential and Kinetic Energy.

The way to open to the Source can only be done by actually making your Mind, Body, Spirit and/or Soul open to the Source by various methods. Open means to quite literally decrease and/or delete the Mental, Physical, Spiritual and Soul Blockages in the Matter and Energy 3D Matrix Complex which is your whole Being. This way you can, without causing too much stress, strain, damage and/or destruction, channel and/or funnel Energy from its multiple sources. This is not easy and requires a lot of personal training on a daily basis equivalent, if not surpassing, that of a 32nd degree + Black Belt Martial Artist. You will then do Mental Acrobat's and also at some point not fail in the ancient Eastern Technique of lifting an object off a table or influencing the flame of a candle.

The trouble is no one Nulls enough, no one practices enough, cause no one has time to do so.

Did not Pythagoras also state that Leisure Time is the key to all Philosophy's?

There has to be a free flow of Energy from the Source through you and/or around you. The only difference with Divine Magic is Priest's and Priestesses who call it from above, unless they are evil from below, through their Deity.

Method's to open to the Sources Of Energy:

You have to have a healthy Body, Mind, Spirit and/or Soul. Blockages, like a twisted spine, prevent such Energy from flowing.

You have to fast now and then. Not eating, or eating only fruit or raw salads, rids the body of the dense, toxic, sludge heap of acquired waste which persists in every cell of your body.

You have to be well nourished, not malnourished. Energy does not flow through degeneration, weakness, dis-ease. Very few agree anymore with extreme Eastern practices of self-torture, nor did Buddha.

You have to be strong and fit. Fit is Fitness, thus working the body to more balance rather than imbalance through poor or extreme habits, where the bones, muscles, tissues, membranes, cells and neurons are not weak, disturbed, damaged, interfering, restricting, crushing and deleting each other.

Avoid extreme conditions like poor posture, severe under/over-weight, sicknesses, diseases, habits, addictions and so forth.

As you can see, all Body first, for first you must prepare the actual vessel to conduct such Energy's and this has been forgotten since Pythagoras. The Mind, or mental faculties, also work at a fraction of their efficiency when weak, sick and/or diseased.

Well, good luck, as they say the Druid Training alone is 10 years.

How long to become a Jedi?

Energy does not flow through irregular or broken structures.

When you first succeed at these you will at that time, by Nature, be ready to learn the techniques to Control Energy, to work Magic.

Control of Magic:

Increasing awareness of your Senses, thus Buddha Awareness of your environment. These are what you have and pick up on many sensations. This leads to your sixth sense, Intuition. Also, if you are just numb and dumb, do you really expect to be able to wield any Form of Energy?

Discipline your Mind, Body, Spirit and/or Soul. You have to be able to focus your Will for any duration of time and on any act you want. Without Discipline there is no Focus, without Focus there is no Will. Without Will there is no Magic. See Zen-Buddhism and most Martial Art's.

You have to learn the Law's Of Nature, thus in all Religion's, Philosophy's and Sciences, preferably do not drop Math cause what Mage does not know Math, the Law's which govern the entire Universe and all aspects of Energy Behavior. This is done through Observation and Experience.

Therefore, yes, also read as much as you possibly can about everything. Entertainment in Video, Film's and Movies is never the same as the Knowledge which you get from books.

When you Master those you will learn, by Nature, the techniques like stated above.

No one said it was easy. Nor should it be.

If you fail, like I have so many times, then know the only difference between those who make it and those who just die is Never Give Up, Never Give Up The Hope.

The reason Magic is even necessary for Human Evolution is we are destined for the Stars.

Conclusion

Most Human's are in a continual Quest to make the Unknown into the Known. To progress beyond the womb and cradle of Mother Earth and into the Great Unknown of Space, we grow beyond what we were before. There is both the path of Science and the path of Magic, the future towards Nature and the one towards Technology, they can even be hand-in-hand. From the cradle we crawl, hop, walk, climb, fly and then curving our backward flowing wings we blast on through to the entire Universe.

What better way to explore and discover the Unknown in the Universe, but naked.

Increasing Self-Consciousness

Introduction

Nowadays, all people have too much stress, emotional conflicts and unhappiness in their lives. Meditation is an ancient method but does not always help. It, however, can help with a lot of things like increasing your Self-Consciousness.

Part 01
Meditation

Let us begin with what Meditation is according to the International Dictionary of Religion: Meditation is clearing the mind of all earthly concerns, often through practical formulae such as set postures, rules of breathing of specific stages of thought in order to allow the individual to concentrate on the absolute, the self, in hope that the higher stage of spiritual awareness will be reached. (Richard Kennedy, The International Dictionary of Religion, pg. 122).

Such a definition sounds good. On the whole it is vague. Meditation is a tool for relaxation, for attaining purer perception and for purging the blocks of Self-Consciousness. No other method achieves these qualities as effectively.

But what methods or types of Meditation are there? My favorite is Kayot-Sarga, a lying Meditation which relaxes every part of the body from toe to head with regulated breathing. I try to do this every time before I fall asleep. You simply lie on your back and relax each and every muscle and joint starting with your right toe and ending in your Crown Chakra while breathing slowly and regularly and clearing your mind of all thoughts and babbling. This helps not only to sleep better but can stimulate Lucid Dreaming.

There are many types of Meditation techniques, especially from the East.

Relaxation

Relaxation and staying calm, alert and relaxed at all times through continuous practice of Buddhistic Observation and Awareness is getting harder and harder to do in Modern Society. According to some statistics even a third of the entire population of Netherlands has suffered post over-stress burn out syndrome…

Through relaxation, our nervous system can become less nervous. Scientific investigation shows a change in electrical brain wave activity. When one meditates to relax, Alpha Waves are produced (Margaret Hatcher, Thinking Through The Essay, Whole Brain Thinking, pg. 80).

Their calm soothing rhythm, their long wave pattern, induces control over an otherwise autonomic nervous system. Regular practitioners can produce Alpha Waves at will. The relaxing result creates a balanced function in the Mind and Body. Bodily stability is quite invaluable, even more so for the Mind. It helps the Spirit and Soul, too. Modern Society generates primarily sharp, rapid, fast waves, especially in a busy City.

What better condition than bodily stability for the function of the mental processes? Even less traffic accidents would be caused. One needs stability in making decisions. One needs even better Observation and Awareness. Without control and calmness the thought process is haywire. Instead of having many conflicting thought patterns, thus a lack of clarity, Meditation gives efficient, energy saving thought process. The brain according to recent scientific research shows that the brain actually uses the most energy of the whole body.

Stressful events cause even more usage by the brain.

With Meditation and Relaxation you will not only improve your life but decision making will be easier, less stressful and more productive.

Part 02
The Best Perception

'The more microscopic attention becomes the more macrocosmic its experience.' (Viktoras H. Kulvinskas, Survival Into The 21st Century, Planetary Healer's Manual, pg. 137).

When we pause for a second in our bustle of activity, and rest for a moment, there is a chance to become aware of our own thoughts. How many are really aware and/or in control of their own thoughts? Do you even notice all the things, all the primarily meaningless things, going through your head in one hour? The complexity found there, the lack of stillness, the chaotic mumble jumble, the unending emotions, all the hectic confusion. There is Chaos dominating.

Meditation, Relaxation, Observation and Awareness distills confusion into harmonious simplicity and promotes the Best Perception. Best Perception is analogous to the optimal performance of an Athlete winning in the Olympics. The Alpha Waves break down the network of crisscrossing speedways going anywhere. The Mind is returned to the owner.

With continued practice there is a distillation from the collective existence of many minds in one, to the one whole mind. This is useful. One can have clarity of thought. The whole of Nature can potentially be seen without bias (as one of the minds see it) and with far greater Objectivity. Practically no one is objective enough. With this pure perception we can have a much better understanding of our lives and existence. It helps us step back and achieve the objective overview, the whole forest rather than focusing continuously on only one tree. This pure perception is not an impossibility as Meditation shows us. Some even go as far to say, like Buddha himself, that we can even gain Enlightenment through Meditation but there is unfortunately very little evidence or proof to back such up.

The Increasing Of Our Self-Consciousness

Meditative introspection helps us to be more Self-Conscious and self-determined beings, rather than thrown to and fro with the emotional wind. We become more Self-Conscious. Little is missed

…and we wake up in Hal Dollig Land again, woo hoo! Boing, boing, boing. Goodbye to the Year of The Cute Little Happy Bunny Rabbit's bouncing everywhere…

and we awake, open-eyed for the first time. Through breaking down old wave patterns, new views reach the mind. We become even more Self-Conscious. Before you know you are having one Gnosis after another. The rotting cesspool of old grey highly repeated images becomes a high resolution vibrant radiance of originality. Our values and deeds change direction, you can even kick a habit. Not just a dog… You start to head towards Truth and Purity, not just unending denial and so many little white lies. You start to move towards as far as your potential allows.

So many people do not believe anymore they can put their life on a new path or get out of an old self-destructive one. I, myself, being a Pisces can talk from Experience too, not just theoretical moralistic lame advice: Having reached 41 now, I have been addicted to almost each and every habit you can think up, Pisces are known for their habits… And equally, I have also had to try about every herb, medicine and medication in the book just to make up for all the shit, trouble and emotional conflicts I have been through with myself and others. However, Pisces are also known for being able to break each habit like it's lemonade, thus such is now also the case and after multiple hospital experiences I enjoy mostly only beer or wine with cigarettes or shag with films…

Sound invented? Not. How many similar stories have you heard from many other…

Ultimately, Meditation strives for the cleansing of all the confusion. This, eventually, after years of practice leads to even heightened perception and cognition. Whether it is taken to this extent is determined by the practitioner. It is a tool there for those willing and able enough to use it.

Again, some go as far as to say we can even go through the so-called Door's Of Perception into other World's through Lucid Dream's and Out-Of-Body Travel, also known as remote viewing, but there is very little evidence or proof to back such up…

It is similar to the unsurmountable problem of trying to bring evidence or proof back from the After Life…

Meditation can also be understood through the study of Neuro-Endocrinology, the study of the ductless glands whereby F.O.F. mechanisms are begun. F.O.F. stands for Fight Or Flight. This is our internal instinct and reaction when faced with a stressful situation i.e. being challenged. It is automatic. Unfortunately, it is reactionary, defying what a calm and controlled Human Being is most of the time: Anger, Fear, Pride, Arrogance, Hate, Deceit and Conceit respectively connected to the hormones secreted by the Gonads, Pancreas, Adrenal, Thyroid, Pituatory and Pineal. (J.S. Zaveri, Preksha Meditation, An Introduction, pg. 19).

With the increase of study in Neurology, Science is also discovering these associations not that they have per se lined it up exactly the same way though it is not impossible when you look at it… It would also be interesting to associate positive emotions.

Further investigation is needed in this area. My own experience with Doctor's has shown me to date a primarily Trial and Error system for medicines and medications; this is not good for the patient who can literally suffer for years with awful side effects and no results or cure in sight...

There is no limit to the extent of Human folly with these Endocrines wild and untamed. It can even explain every last teenage behavior. Our glands are closely connected to our Chakras and the 7 listed above are from your Base Chakra to your Crown Chakra.

Through Meditation the nature of our Being is brought into light. Our automatic reactions, normally presenting themselves in the most grievous ways, will be tempered until clarified. This is the strength of Meditation.

Conclusion

This is when Human becomes Master of the Temple. The Temple is the Body. The Body should be in obedience to the Mind, not vice versa. With mastery, the meaningful reasoning of a Self-Conscious Mind can shine. Light on issues never before seen can be understood. No more must we move around blinded by Pain and Strife and Rage. We can open up to new views, ditch old programming, dump emotional baggage, delete floating garbage and become a new Self-Conscious Human mastering the Temple Body.

What an incredible tool and so easy to practice... Whether Meditation actually does deliver all of these awards over time one can only find out oneself...

The Conundrum Solution

Materialism, Interactionism and Idealism in the Mind/Body Problem hold positions which are extreme. Each has some Truth to them and some Lie. So it is with all things extreme.

The terms Mind, Body, Thought, Idea, Intellect, Materialism, Interactionism and Idealism hold meanings for us which deceive us. The theory which I hope to propose here is a more generic way of explaining how we operate.

When we look at ourselves we see Body. Body to us is something which can be sensed. When we ask who and/or what is looking we have a tougher time. What is perceiving the Body? What is conceiving the Body? Who am I? There is much confusion in this area, because that which is perceiving cannot be sensed. The I is not measurable by any known device or method. It is unfortunately therefore quite impossible to determine what it is through such, since there is no way of perceiving it. This, of course, includes the fact there is also no way of demonstrating it to others what it may be.

When I look in a mirror I see only what I look like, not who I am.

Also, by the very logic that I am perceiving, I cannot perceive that which is perceiving.

Philosopher's, Psychologist's and Scientist's are left with the futile effort of determining and demonstrating that which has never been seen, touched, or felt, that which has never been determined or demonstrated.

So a pitfall if the arguing of pointless Dogmas, saying only that which can be seen, touched, or felt is True. The result is the worst kind of Materialism imaginable, now also dominating the entire Modern Western Civilization at the beginning of the 21st Century. The result is also close-mindedness and the denial of other realities: Conception was never good for accuracy and Perception is highly relative.

What is needed is increased Observation and Experience so we may come across more evidence, more proof and new methodologies which are capable of determining and demonstrating, using the Scientific Method, the I.

There is no other way to prove the I, just as with all other axioms, if we cannot preferably show it on a computer screen then forget it, it is a fantasy, a figment of our imagination and we enter a far greater crisis than ever before in Reality Theory's.

Example: We operate on many levels. The question is, where do those actions stem from? What is the trunk and what are the roots? The trunk would be the medium and the roots would be the causes, the leaves and fruit are the result.

Since the trunk is invariably connected to the roots, the cause and medium are never separated. Looking at the way we behave in this manner is more applicable and sensible than by flailing about with Dogmas, Mind, Body, Thought, Idea, Intellect, Materialism, Interactionism and Idealism: All are floating in abstract space with no concrete definitions, evidence and/or proof which have never been thoroughly dealt with by the Scientific Method. Such things have also never been shown on any screen, the best to date is vague electron and neuro transfers through veins and brain nerves; learning is apparently no more than the growth of a neural path...

Where is Memory, though? Everyone is still divided on this one.

So, we have to go about this in a different way, rather than being trapped in only Materialistic Biological Science.

Since we know what our actions are, most people know what they are actually doing, we can then explore from where they came from through logical progression of Cause and Effect. By analyzing the actions and their cause, we can figure out why and from where they came about. By knowing where and why, we can possibly then figure out how. How is a tough question but also the most important question. Without the how we can do nothing. With the source of your action answered, and the cause of its birth under hat, how it came about is practically fully answered.

Example: If one can follow a causal chain through a Timeline from Point A. Cause and Point Z Result through thousands of variables then we can possibly generate enough evidence and proof about the question to gain an almost certain answer.

Such example is also not in denial of the Scientific Method, it simply applies such to our very lives and histories...

In this way, systems become practical and not dogmatic. The System, and any system to answer any question, The Conundrum Solution, becomes practical and not only theoretical. Confusion, single-mindedness and extremism are shed. The primarily theoretical nature of most Scientific Theory's with very heavy based dependence on Materialism and Mathematic's falls away. Useful application is gained. This is the essence of The Conundrum Solution. This is the key to Knowledge and Information and learning and progression and Evolution. This is the part which counts and which underlies all Unknown's.

Example: Everyone has Intuition, therefore Intuition exists. Everyone describes Intuition as some type of foresight through a feeling, premonition or vision therefore that is what Intuition is.

One does not even need to prove such on a computer screen. It is also by the Law Of Repetition of evidence and proof through the Scientific Method not invalid.

One can also argue that demonstrating and determining something to only 3 Scientist's in white coats in a lab 3 times over is no proof at all! Next to the controlled environment, you also need the test environment and many more experiments.

Instead of denying the whole world and reality, and all our common experiences, instead of arguing impossibly extreme positions, each Philosopher and Scientist should work on what they know into a working whole. Eventually, through such methods the Unknown becomes the Known.

Once we repeat it for ourselves and our group on a daily basis we do not even need some white coat to tell us it is true. We are merely practicing such scientific principles and methods through Observation and Experience to each and every last aspect of our lives.

Especially the invisible ones, such simply means Unknown at this time.

Each of us becomes a regular practitioner of the art of Observation and Experience and we apply it to our lives to answer each and every last conceivable question and to reach any Known or Unknown Reality.

This is also theoretically the Path To Enlightenment and Immortality for such concepts require the Unknown to become the Known. It could even be the Holy Grail…

However, I keep asking, do you need to know only one branch or the whole tree?

Once we can determine and demonstrate each and every last fact and truth in entire existence through The Conundrum Solution then, maybe, eternal hopeless incessant purely theoretical hopeless debate, which is cramping and hindering all fields of study due to their unending argument of 'no evidence' and 'no proof', will cease. I can also add that mere dismissal is no attempt at a solution.

No evidences? No proofs? Nonsense. Look all around you… and in each of you… see all the commonalities… Truth is Commonality.

The Only Constant Is Change

Introduction

'Everything is relative from the point-of-view of the observer.' Albert Einstein.
'Maybe it is.
Maybe it is not.
Maybe it is and is not.
Maybe it is indescribable.
Maybe it is and is indescribable.
Maybe it is and is not and is indescribable.' Jainism.

The second quote is the many sidedness of Reality as presented by Jainism, an Eastern Religious Science with its own roots dating back to India 4000 B.C. It is also closely tied in with tolerance and non-violence, 'Ahimsa': Compassion for all living beings. It sums up all the possible points of views. It is a valuable statement and value for going through life because it demands open-mindedness.

Life is full of permutations. Richard Bach's, Illusion's, The Adventures of a Reluctant Messiah explains how to go about facing everything. To understand what something really is, when one encounters it, one must first know from what Point Of View one is looking from.

A Point Of View is the culmination of all the things which you are and/or are not at the Point in Time you observe something. This determines what you sense, how you interpret it and how you react to it, often without first thinking...

Part 01
Interpenetration

We are in the 4ᵗʰ Dimension, Space and Time, as purported by Science and the vast majority of all other Religion's and Philosophy's. In the Dimension of Space and Time the force of Cause and Effect rules. Cause and Effect are true as proven by each and everything we do. Each and every Cause and Effect is a transfer of Energy and as Newton stated, 'Each and every action has an equal and opposite reaction' and not by some vague philosophical abstract notion but by the Law's Of Physic's themselves.

Also by the Law of Transformation and Conservation of Energy each and everything is Energy.

Once again as stated by Albert Einstein: 'We may therefore regard matter as being constituted by the regions of space in which the field is extremely intense. There is no place in this new kind of physics both for the field and matter, for the field is the only reality.' Static Matter therefore does not exist: Matter is only bundles of Energy.

The way in which this Energy dances together makes it appear real in a certain way to us, dependent on our Point Of View, like The Table Paradox. Even though I retorted the Table Paradox quite well I still did not deny your own perception as modifying your experience of Reality. Energy is the movement of the substances and Matter is the density of the field, if you interpret Einstein literally, therefore also a measure of how real it is to us.

This is also shown by the Eastern Mystical word of 'Interpenetration'. Since Energy exists on many levels, Scientist's have gone down to sub-atomic levels, and since Matter made by bundles of Energy, what we know, sense and are is a measure of how deep we have penetrated and become conscious of such realities. This is demonstrated by Science even: At one time Scientist's knew of only Electron's and Proton's. They explored deeper and found the Nucleus, the explored deeper and found the sub-atomic world. Sub-atomic particles are particles within Atom's. Particles are dynamic patterns of Energy since particles are bundles of Energy = Matter. Therefore, the World and Universe and Reality is one big dynamic pattern of Energy within another dynamic pattern of Energy, within another and so on.

Due to our nanoscopic mortal Human Point Of View and our limited consciousness and this stage of our development and the Evolution of Humanity primarily Illusion and Delusion reigns with Ignorance dominating. Another great quote, this time by Socrates himself: 'The only sin is ignorance.'

And most certainly not the Christian 'Ignorance is Bliss'. If Ignorance is such bliss then why is it the cause of all evil, strife, sickness and disease on Planet Earth? Or, if I know how to and can free myself then why would I suffer anymore?

We understand things well or poorly dependent on how much we have found out and discovered things from our Individual or Collective Point Of View i.e. me reading a book or going on Internet. In other words, how deep we have interpenetrated into the external and internal worlds.

'Films about living on this planet about living on other planets; anything that's got space and time is all movie and all Illusion,' he said, 'But for a while we can learn a huge amount and have a lot of fun with our Illusions, can we not?' <u>Richard Bach, The Adventures of a Reluctant Messiah</u>.

This Theory demands Life to be constantly changing in Form. Life does change Form. It also states Reincarnation, by such above stated Law's of Physic's themselves even, is at least feasible and definitely not completely impossible. Energy is in all ways interchanging and interacting, thus interpenetrating. Energy forms Matter and vice versa, thereby we are complex Energy Form's.

What is contradicting the possibility of changing your present Form into another Form? Form, after all, is a matter of interpretation.

It is also a Matter of Interpenetration.

Part 02
Cause and Effect

To repeat: We are in the 4ᵗʰ Dimension, Space and Time, as purported by Science and the vast majority of all other Religion's and Philosophy's. In the Dimension of Space and Time the force of Cause and Effect rules. Cause and Effect are true as proven by each and everything we do. Each and every Cause and Effect is a transfer of Energy and as Newton stated, 'Each and every action has an equal and opposite reaction' and not by some vague philosophical abstract notion but by the Law's Of Physic's themselves.

Still though, within String Theory and the to date discovered dimensions as I proposed in a recent Essay, it is still highly debatable as to whether or not Time is actually the 12ᵗʰ dimension and not the 4ᵗʰ Dimension. 4 is coincidentally evenly divisible through 12 but all the entire clock and calendar is based on a 12, 24, 60 system.

'We buy tickets to these films, paying admission by agreeing to believe in the reality of space and the reality of time… Neither one is true but anyone who does not want to pay that price cannot appear on this planet or in any space-time system at all.' Richard Bach, The Adventures of a Reluctant Messiah.

Richard Bach is ultimately saying it's up to you to choose your Destiny, Fate, Effect, Karma by enacting your right and will to Choose and Cause your own future. He is also saying you have to have paid that admission fee to be in the Cause and Effect Space Time Realm, the Material Plane Of Existence.

Jain's would say you have formed yourself and are here due to your Karma and the Energy you have put into things and yourself which now Effect your Life, through multiple Reincarnation's, and which will continue to Cause it and events in it.

Scientist's would say every Effect has a Cause, something which should be applied a lot more in Medical Science who are very heavily only symptom based with the diagnose and prescription of medicines.

Philosopher's would say there is a Past, Present and Future, all interconnected through Cause and Effect through multiple Timelines.

Many other Religion's, Judaism, Christianity and Islam, also have a very strong sense of Moral's, Values and Good and/or Evil. Though they have difficulty admitting such in various interpretations even Christianity has their own sense of Karma.

The best example from Christianity is phrased two ways: 'That which is done unto you shall be done unto others.' or 'Do unto others as they have done unto you.'

Quite different implications, yet meaning the same Law of Cause and Effect, for you can theoretically be the vessel or instrument of your God, Goddess or GOD not that Human has enough Intelligence and Wisdom to 'get even' or 'take revenge' or 'find retribution' or 'grant justice on their heads'.

Karma is not some stupid primitive foolish Human taking the law into his or her own hands… Karma is a Law of the Universe which through Cause and Effect governs all things.

The trouble though, why does it always take so long to activate? Some Types of Karma, especially if you have not resolved such by the time you reach your death bed, go onto the next

Life. Thus, practically by definition alone with support of the Law's of the Universe, Karma is a necessity.

Without such Order, everything would dissolve into Chaos and my mere desire decides the fate of your entire Civilization. Well, there is your bloody warfare throughout the entire History of Humanity. In almost each and every case it is also practically determined by petty, and sometimes not so petty, Dictator's.

Except for the French Revolution and the Slave Revolution the vast majority of such Warfare and War's have not been determined, or decided, by the People.

Each Field, so to speak, is actually saying the same thing.

'A Rose by any other name, still remains the same...' Shakespeare.

After all, Energy underlies us all, each and everything, and is governed by the Absolute Law of Cause and Effect.

Conclusion

A wonder it is at what point in the Past we made the choices to be what we are now. A mystery at what in GOD's name possessed us...

A great wonder it is, through the Tabla Rasa Effect since we do not remember, what choices we made in a Past Life and how we wonder and wander around angry and sorrowful as to why we suffer so much on a daily basis.

We can never seem to find our Peace and/or Freedom and longing for more and more and better and better...

'Be grateful for what you have.'

'You do not know what you got until it is gone.'

'The grass is always greener on the other side.'

Each is a commonly known proverb. Yet, the actual underlying Quantum Law's Of Physic's and consequences for our beliefs, interpretations and definitions of our existence in Reality, in all Field's of Science, Philosophy and Religion, are far reaching.

'Think before you act.'

'Do only what is first carefully considered.'

'Practice more wisdom in your valor.'

This is the biggest Lesson of Karma, how each of our lives go up or down, towards Good or Evil, success or disaster: Responsibility.

Responsibility, the strongest aspect of Cause and Effect, in one's thoughts, words and actions is a Cardinal Principle of Jainism and many other primarily moralistic and ethical based systems. Responsibility demands careful attention to your own Cause and Effect's, something we rarely observe and stay aware of, with you the creator, the one causing your life, the one in control of your future as the center of attention.

'You are the maker of your own Fate.'

'There is no Fate but your own.'

'You cannot escape your own Fate.'

Responsibility for your Past, Present and Future in direct relation to the Law of Cause and Effect in each and every part of your internal and external realities puts you as the one in control: You are a small creator, a manipulator of Energy. You do this each minute of the day by your very motion and as you see fit. You are ultimately, by such Law's and Definition's, and the very fact you exist, the one in control, or as in most cases randomly and emotionally on every whim and desire steering your vessel straight downwards at a minus 90 degree highway completely blind with no steering wheel and the hyper acceleration effect completely off the scale…

You are ultimately the one causing, no matter how out of control you may seem: 'Within each of us lies the power of our consent to health and to sickness, to riches and to poverty and to freedom and to slavery. It is we who control these, and not another.' <u>Richard Bach, The Adventures of a Reluctant Messiah</u>.

Thus, thank GOD, we really are relatively nanoscopic in the entire Universe. Go to the top of the Universe again, look down, and presto Planet Earth has completely disappeared…

What is wrong with this picture?

For how far greater and larger the Idealism and Spirit and Soul of Humanity really is.

For some, indeed, it is quite heavenly and for others so very hellish.

Light Wave And Particle Emission's

Emission's and States

Waves = Emissions.

Particles = States.

It repeats ad infinitum.

Observer Camera through inanimate object causes EM Wave Interference - In front of screen with two splits.

What happens with the Observer Camera behind the screen where Electron's are shot through? Do they know?

Therefore, why does it who Particle Behavior with Observer Camera?

This EM Interference causes Wave Cancellations.

Does the the second and third screens with 2 splits and 5 splits also cause Wave Cancellation?

With two cameras: Impact of Electron's causes Wave Emission; Electron's follow EM Wave by Attraction with Wave Interference and causes brighter spots which line up with points on second screen.

With both wave and electron because of Maxwell's EM Gravity Theory which forces it to follow such laws.

Non-Local Interference

Two particles across a greater distance can have Non-Local Interference or Non-Local Causal Factor.

Information has no Mass thus causes same Particle States instantaneously at any distance.

The geometrical 3D Form travels.

Schrodinger's Cat Theory states that by all probability and possibilities the Universe could be the shape of a cat.

A single atom has 100^{30} possibilities.

A calculation of 10 electrons and their wave functions overlapping has to be calculated.

It is State and Emission.

There is no confusion, only for the Observer!

Energy Form's

Our cognitive perception and will can change Reality. At least, Reality as we Observe and Experience it.

It can even change water particles as proven by Japanese studies.

The difference, therefore, between Good and Evil is the combination of Light Energy and Dark Energy. Thus, also Light Matter and Dark Matter.

We are each more complex versions of the basic Sine Wave: The Form's are the electrons and atoms in States and the wave is the emission of Energy and Information.

The Universe is not flat; the other dimensions make up the whole spherical Universe. The Matter being heavier could be pulled more inwards as concerted by Scientist's who tend to be overly materialistic with their instruments of measurement seeing only the Material Body's.

The Universe is a multi-dimensional web-like matrix where all things are interconnected through such EM Wave Particle Interference through interaction, attraction, repulsion, collision and emission. The entanglement utilizes massless transfer of Information. Information is only limited by the medium. Information must therefore be differentiating states in different configurations and associations i.e. a shape Apple or Orange is recognized.

The Big Bang Theory demands a spherical Universe for all things expand in all directions. First extreme Chaos then there is stabilization. The confusion arises from 'flat' states and 'excited' states. The expansion is at the same speed in all directions into Nothingness and Nothing.

The center of the Universe would therefore be the only non-moving point in Space Time. This could be a Null Point or a GOD Particle. It could also collapse back on itself.

For references read Schrodinger, Heisenberg, Einstein, Newton, Planck and others. Or just grab a whole bunch of recent Scientific American's.

Evolutionary Essays – Epilogue
My Life Commandment's

Poetry Ad Infinitum 'n Defens Ad Absurdum

To become a Global Person just take the best Element's of each Culture or Nation: There is never only one Species, Race or Nation.

Without a Sense Of Humor, one can never, survive, live, or thrive…

An opening is thinner than a window, a window is thinner than a door, and a door is thinner than a wall…

Money can never be the ONLY motivation…

All Thing's are in Motion; Time does not Exist; Time is confused with Motion.

Reality is Virtuality's within Virtuality's and/or is Reality's within Reality's in One Big Reality and/or Both.

You can never make it being ONLY self-motivated.

1. Earth 6. Shadow 2. Water 7. Light 3. Air 8. Form 4. Fire 9. Spirit 5. Ether 10. Soul

Null Clock null clock null Clock Null clock NULL CLOCK null CLOCK NULL clock

Beyond Duality: Each Form possesses various quantities and qualities which are perceived as Good and/or Neutral and/or Evil, dualistic, by Human's and other Life Form's. It's actually just about a change in Form with quantities and qualities.

The Way To The Future is through clean renewable Sources Of Energy.

Equal In Return (The Fact You Lack It You Are Attracted).

Not Equal In Return: Karma has a 1X to 10X to 100X to 1000X Magnification Factor.

If you kick a Dog then why does a Horse show up and kick you in the head sending you flying back at 266 km/h into a Tree? Dog's cannot kick, they only know how to wipe their poopie clean on the grass with their back legs. A transformation of the Object takes place in Karma, but not always. A House Karma can turn into a House Karma.

Both Instances = True. Instances = English Sentence A AND English Sentence B. You can translate it if you want, now, but good luck cross-referencing.

If there is not some daily pleasure in Life than Life is not worth living.

Their definition of Free Speech is more like Free For All Mode. Insulting everyone under the Sun of Allah is NOT Free Speech.

Having NO Rules and/or Law's is NOT Freedom and/or Peace.

Try to escape from the System…

When an honest hard working Human does not get paid and/or appreciated and/or rewarded for his Work then there will be Evil and/or Retribution and/or Revenge and/or Retaliation and/or Rebellion and/or Resistance and/or Revolution.

Good is Evil: Your Enemy is Evil to me but my Enemy is Good to you.

Genius is Insane: The greatest Weapon Of Mass Destruction, the Null Bomb Planet Exploder launched into the Magma Core of a Sun, Planet or Moon, can also be used to save Humanity against an Alien Invasion.

However, GOD ≠ SATAN otherwise there is no Free Will and no Good and/or Neutral and/or Evil in Reality.

Ys us os is vs es as...

When a Human has no right to Defend his Home then it is truly End Of World's.

'The Heights To Which One Man Can Fall.' said the Radio Broad Caster.

© KLP

Tulip's, Monitor's and Screen's

The Free Show © Kyle Lance Proudfoot © Kyle Lans Proudfoot

My name was translated at my Birth in Toronto, Canada, Planet Earth, Milky Way Galaxy by my Mother, M.H. Lans.

Do I therefore have a Pen Alias my whole Life and does it cause any copyright, intellectual property and/or ownership Issues?

AKA's: 1. Silver, High Wizard 2. Silber, Psionic Warlock 3. Revlis, Vampire Demon 4. Mr. Newbie, Rules Lawyer 5. Roary, Fire Dragon.

The Elite Isolated Spaceship: Do Not talk to me. Do Not talk about me. Do Not associate with me. Do Not approach me. Do Not ask me. Do Not FM respond. Do Not DE me. Do Not DOS me. Do Not terrorize me. Do Not do me. Do Not InterAct™ with me. Do Not Spy Stalk me. Do Not Relate to me.

What is wrong with you people? Are you unwell?

Are you Bwain Damaged? How many 'w's' do you have in your Bwain Damage, now?

Maybe you should check yourself, go wreck yourself, into a Shrink and/or Psychologist and/or Psychiatrist...

Or, you're gonna get yourself locked up, or Dead, in a Federal Prison.

Yes, so-called Proof and/or Evidence, but I will see everything that has happened to me and everyone near me and what we each did and did not do in the Bardo State and next to GOD, God's and Goddesses, Angel's and Demon's, Hero's and Villain's there is also just the actual binding Karma's.

However, whereas The Elite Isolated Spaceship, cruising through Space And Time with ONLY me, Silber, Psionic Warlock, in it is the ONLY place one can ever realize Utopia, it unknowingly crosses the border of an Alien Territory and it's not as though they're about to put up signs in the middle of Space saying its theirs... And then Alien's show up out of nowhere and blow your Space Ship to Kingdom Come.

They think they can deter and/or dissuade me, that's like hitting my Aries at Full Moon: With all the Deflection, Reflection and/or Backfire Effect's going around it's more like Aries shows up and stomps your entire Country.

The Green Activist is not a Green Terrorist, Green Hacker, Green Killer, Tree Killer, Plant Killer, Animal Killer, Life Killer, Planet Killer, Human Killer, Wife Killer, Job Killer and/or Work Killer. At the rate of consumption across over-population explosion there will be nothing left and no work in a decade.

We drink, eat, smoke, make or break, what is it for life's sake?

To learn, to earn, not always burn, when time eternal turns.

For some inexplicable reason death has to wipe out Humanity on a regular basis.
© Kyle Lance Proudfoot
(Or, do I have to explicitly state Mr. Kyle Lance Proudfoot?)

END

About The Author

I first started in IT in 1997 when I started my website, Silverlingo.com, but I was actually already busy since arcades in Toronto, Canada. From 2001 to 2005 I worked as a system administrator in diverse instances, since then as a webmaster, web designer and/or web developer on about twenty websites. I have also done projects such as writing, editing, and translating text, including publishing five books, making music, art, and B-humor film, plus open source scripting and 2D/3D graphic design. My most recent project, which is also continuous, is my photography and video, which I am busy uploading to Google+.

My passion is writing in genres such as philosophy, science fiction, fantasy, humor, poetry, politics, psychology, and now even in sciences. See also my sister website, Planesofexistence.eu, which is dedicated to my writing.

Next to IT I have a lot of knowledge and work experience in literature, music, art, film, 3D games, Internet, multimedia, entertainment, and social media to develop projects independently or with others to make open source to retail products. So far over three decades I have done thirty-thousand-plus sessions of the Free Show, watched nine-thousand-plus films, and played most 3D games except the most recent ones.

My goals for the future are to make Literature, film, music, photography, art, video, audio, science fiction, fantasy, humor, poetry, philosophy, psychology, politics, space travel, the Free Show, biking, nature, 3D games, cooking.